I0510653

SCOD ECONOMICS

Alternative Economic Theories

Author: Drogo Empedocles
Editor: Walton D. Stowell II
2017 Edition: 2

*

A book about alternative economic theory using ecological ethics, with some erotic foreplay.

*

SCOD Economics; Alternative Economic Theories

Economics affects everyone, even those that do not want to be concerned with money or finances. This book is a summary of alternative economic commentaries that emphasize democratic ethics. The Sustainable Cooperative for Organic Development believes in valuing human lives as responsible environmental stewards for our biosphere called Earth, and seeks ways to allow for biodiversity in civilization as well as the ecosystem. We believe in less monopolies, less corporate crony politics, less corruption in government, and more ways to support various ways of life and provide future generations with the ability to provide for themselves. Please let's work together to leave something for the children that is worth inheriting.

*

Sexological Sexonomix Foreplay

Forward by an Erotic Ecological Romance Writer

Brittany was intrigued by Jack. She couldn't help but visualize touching his lips with every sweet word that cascaded from them. They reached the top of the stairs and he turned to her, both laughing in a childlike way. Brittany grabbed his shoulder for some stability and bent over, still laughing, trying to catch her breath. She looked up toward Jack, and was taken aback by the way the light caught his eyes- almost as in how the twinkle of a distant star can sometimes appear in the night sky. She held her breath for a moment and Jack grabbed her and pulled her in close. The feeling of his lips pressed against hers sent shock-waves through her body. He tasted like a warm breeze in spring-time. He leaned down and gently kissed her neck and her hardened nipples began to push even harder through her blouse as she brushed against his warm body. She couldn't deny the throbbing she felt between her moistened thighs, lusciously synchronized with each beating of her heart.

In closer he pulled her, his swollen man-hood pressed tightly inside his pants and against her leg; and she wanted more than ever to feel him sink inside of her love. His roaming hands traced her neckline, and found their way to the buttons on her blouse. One by one he undid them, and followed each revelation of her skin with a tender kiss. They danced their way in embracing arms toward the bed, where they landed with him on top of her, his lips still navigating her ever exposing body. She adjusted herself for a moment, allowing the blouse to fall gracefully from her arms, and Jack slid it gently down the rest of the way and threw it to the side of the bed. His strong hands now finding their way to her large beautiful breasts that were still hiding under the cloak of her black brassiere. One by one, he slipped his hands under her straps and exposed her gloriously perky tits with exuberance.

2

Jack pulled himself in closer so that he could bury his face into her soft graces. His lip brushed against her bare nipple, and she could feel the heat of his throbbing cock pressing closer in on her thighs, under his pants; and her long gypsy skirt was now starting to ride up her leg. Jack was now suckling on Brittany's tit and she felt her pussy tighten with each flicker of his tongue on her nipple. Her hands found its way up his shirt, where she found his nipples to be just as erect as hers. They broke their embrace only for a second to remove Jack's shirt. Now his bare skin was pressed against hers.

During the brief shirt interlude, the history of Jack's shirt flashed before his mind's eye. He remembered first buying that shirt for his new job at the architecture office. His memories were all so positive during those early days of fountain-head enthusiasm. Jack was so eager to kiss the ass of his bosses and coworkers, he worked hard over-time, wasted weekends to meet deadlines, pulled all-nighters worrying about problems, and ran errands for anyone. Now all those feelings had turned sour, and were making him bitter. Throwing his shirt with such abandon, was now a perfect release of repressed angst.

He was in a new phase of life.

[...to be continued in a SCOD Romance Novel...]

Note from Author: "Regarding introduction prolog pages to books, I feel some forward playing is nice to ease into the harder, more difficult adult content to follow, concerning the World's oldest profession."
XXXOOOXXX

*

Reasons for an Artist Architect to write a book on
Economics & Politics

Wealth inequality is on the rise.

What does that mean for regular people?

Rising wealth inequality nationally means the rich are getting richer, more drastically than before; and the poor are getting poorer, which means they will soon have the rights of displaced Native Americans from 100 years ago. Imagine how that might affect minorities like many blacks and natives who already have the poverty of third-world countries, but are required to pay the fees of first-world plutocrats and corporate cronies?

Most of us are still feeling the Great Recession in our daily lives. The national economic 'growth' data that popular economists use, shows that the corporate bail-out sectors of our economy grew. Can you guess what percentage of our population benefited from that growth? Most of it went to the elite 1%.

Many of us middle-class people are losing our wealth when we try to sell our homes because of mortgage real-estate fraud on the bank's behalf, devaluing old homes in areas of slow growth, and using tax money to build new developments which makes a few rich while we get poorer without as many jobs, because money has been drained from the middle to go to the top.

I remember when I first noticed corporate take-over locally in the 1990's when Walmarts began 'out-competing' all the mom-and-pop small family owned stores, and almost monopolized the market even for large franchise chains. Cable-companies made fortunes stringing wires around the country, into rural areas, competing with 'WV state-flowers' and antenna TV. Larger companies replaced smaller ones, every-where.

It is time to change the system, but it is not 'all or nothing'. There are elements of alternative systems every-where in history, and around us in America today. If we do not have a right to live, our leaders do not have a right to rule, because they enforce the laws that make us unable to provide for ourselves, laws which we need to take responsibility to change.

Power for the people, and by the people is a constant struggle. 'Power to the people'! We have to take the power back, from the plutocrats. Economics and politics are combined in America as a corrupt form of crony 'State Capitalism'. No conspiracy or theory is needed to explain the reality of how corporations function, it is notoriously blatant and commonly accepted as 'just the way things are'; so without defining every popular economic term that Madoff and Greenspan advocated, I will try to high-light the problems that affect most of us, and propose solutions.

"People Power!!!" - *AMM (Appalachian Mountain Militia)*

I do not expect people to take my word as total truth. I want average people to get interested in how our system works, by helping them to feel that they can make a difference simply by beginning to question the establishment in intelligent ways. I am not a professional economist, I am studying finance as a hobby. For this book I am able to put forth theories by several economists, scientists, and philosophers; by rewording or quoting them. There are probably many people that disagree with my opinions, and I will not include all the information that a basic or advanced economic book would; but I will do my best to interpret and phrase jargon with references as best I can.

SCOD Thesis was designed and published in 1999 to address alternative ways to live architecturally. It was mocked by critics as absurd interest in 'commune' village design that was not financed by rich clients, commercial investors, or the government, and silly for having no conventional 'profit' motive.

I accepted the responsibility of revolutionary rebels every-where, and as a system out-cast in college, I began to learn more about business, and got a clearer impression how the corporate world worked. My experience as a college graduate trying to 'earn a living' by selling myself to anyone willing to pay me, was even more discouraging and depressing.

As a drafting assistant, design partner, professor of architecture, and architectural adviser I was so in debt that any money I made had to go directly to pay debt bills, and did not allow me to save for the basics of middle-class property and personal benefit expectations that were promised to come to everyone that played by the rules of the system (higher education = more income). I found those platitudes to be hollow, even for many like me who wanted to find a life-long career within 'good' firms. Well it was clear the world for practicing architects was changing from what it had been. I did work with my father for years, and as partners we completed many designs and built many projects; however we made very little profit.

My father and I were successful designers, but that success did not transfer financially. Part of the reason capitalism did not work for us, was that many clients were poor, and even the rich wanted to save money. My father out of the kindness of his heart and joy to serve others, and enthusiasm for his craft, would charge fees that may have gone further during the 1970s. Combine low pay with the rise in cost of living, inflation, and this is why my mother had to support our family by working commercial retail at Walmart and teaching at schools; both jobs luckily she enjoyed as best she could. I worked many other jobs besides architecture, sometimes 5 jobs a month, and always actively found back-up jobs and projects that kept me busy. Despite only having one family car and very few luxuries for middle-class, we saw our wealth diminish no matter how hard we worked, and no matter how many clients we had.

I lived within my means, on the budget of a lower-class individual, while striving to serve the public as a middle-class citizen educated by 'higher institutions of education'. I did not 'drop-out' of the system, the system was not interested in using me for the purpose that my education, psychology, and skill-set allowed. I still continue to live in this way, which I feel is the best I can do with what I have available to me.

I do not say these things to complain that my family suffered more than lower-class people, or disabled people (who can easily be disenfranchised by society and the system). I am not comparing how we lived to how other classes live, the point of being honest about my middle-class family experience is to show why I believe that alternative economic systems are important. I have always been interested in the definition of economics, and silly questions like "why do we say 'trade & barter' if those terms are synonyms?". My favorite question as a child was "what makes a unit of something worth anything?"; or more humorously "can we just start using bottle caps or shells as money?". I still think those types of questions are good.

Professionals whose books and recordings I studied for this book include Dr. Dean Baker, Prof. Noam Chomsky, Prof. Mark Blyth, Economist Michael Hudson, Professor Wolff, politicians Bernie Sanders, Jill Stein, Jeremy Corbyn, and many others.

Regardless of opinion, it is good to hear that other people suffer from a type of economic exchange we could call the "oops I should have asked for more" syndrome. So I will try to include a few of those stories too for you. Enjoy the most boring theories you never thought might affect you, and keep on keepin' on.

If I understand some economists correctly, they are saying we are living in a period like the 1920s when all growth was in the stock market; it was considered 'capital gain' but was really 'striping assets'; which resulted in the Stock Market Crash and Great Depression. No pressure people (sarcasm).

Jeremy Corbyn in the Labor (Labour) Party in England, makes Bernie Sanders look like a centrist about public policies.

"For the many, not the few." - *Corbyn Labour party platform*

"Our challenge to a rigged system, is bound to meet hostility. Change always involves taking on vested interests. The stakes are very high." - *Jeremy Corbyn, British Labour Party 2017*

Great experimentation with individual and social action must take place now! I have been writing and publishing essays on Teaching, Colleges, Jobs, and systemic economic problems and solutions. In 2017 I am producing a series of recordings and essays on 'SCOD Economics'. This Economic series includes interviews and biographies across disciplines, and intends to address both present injustices and futurist hopes.

We will discuss injustice within our educational and political system, that adversely affects people with alternative thoughts or theories that are not accepted by the conventional establishment corporate ideology frame-work that contains and controls most of the World. We are given their propaganda that "we can all have any job we want, so long as we try hard and get good grades". Our reality based on my experience is more like "most of us can have at least a minimum-wage job with few benefits, for a limited amount of time, without job security, pathetic interest for savings accounts, the job we find may be against our own interests, and those who cannot get good grades or are bad at following orders get nothing and will probably end up in jail or homeless". Despite these problems which I have personally witnessed and experienced, the final goal of the series is to plan for a better more sustainable tomorrow for future generations; even if the series conclusions are largely ignored within our life-times. Historic record has some worth.

*

SCOD Economic Recordings:
Tom the Data Scientist, Libertarian
Beamer the Scientist, Liberal
Aeyla the Care Giver, Independent
Scorpion the Homeless, Democrat
Drogo the Architect, Green
My Favorite Job Was Teaching
How Crony-Capitalism Affects Education
Homeless Ways of Life
Public Art & Street Teaching
Alternative Economic Education
Graduate School Politics in Colleges & University
Permaculture in Economics, Business, & Politics
Quest For Consciousness - MD University
Jimmy Dore & Mark Blyth Economix
'The World Is An Angry Place' - Trump

*

What is the difference between Trade & Barter?
The terms are synonyms, but trade more commonly refers to the transaction of goods or services (commodities) often involving stocks or money (currency). Barter connotes negotiation or haggling between people seeking to exchange one commodity for another. Trade and barter can be swapped one for the other.

World Trade Organization
"There are a number of ways of looking at the World Trade Organization. It is an organization for trade opening. It is a forum for governments to negotiate trade agreements. It is a place for them to settle trade disputes. It operates a system of trade rules. Essentially, the WTO is a place where member governments try to sort out the trade problems they face with each other." - *from WTO website*

*

Conspiracy Theories are Stupid
((Double-Speak Snark Edition))

It is very popular to debunk 'factoids', and label what we consider 'false' as stupid 'conspiracy theories'. It is always popular to consider party ideas, as 'the truth' of reality because it is apparent to peers. Society continues to under-go this process of determining cultural meaning, as scientific 'belief' and religious 'faith' often divide along voting lines. Climate Change is real to one part in the 2-party system, and fake for the second party. The most difficult issues in history, seem to divide populations down the center, with the Nation (like in the Civil War) broken with fanatical duality. One side emerges publicly as the winners after a war or major political action, even if the other side is still virtually equal in numbers if not power.

One thing to remember is that an under-ground economy always exists, it is often called 'the black-market' comprised of double-agents, criminals, mafias, and gangs. Also it is publicly known as a fact that we have secret military and spy branches in government, often called 'black-ops' comprised of the FBI, CIA, NSA, and others. For most of society, these powerful entities may as well be considered conspiracy theories by the general population, with no real existence in their every-day lives or careers, much like politics.

"How do the elites control General Motors? Why isn't that a question? It is because GM is an institution of the elites, they don't have to control it, they own it." - *Noam Chomsky*

My favorite job was teaching college in She-town. That job was taken away from me, by a conservative Dean who was in bed with the Coal Company in southern WV. Despite my father and I teaching for low wages (2 for 1 deal), and being successful at educating our students who enjoyed our classes because we shared knowledge rather than tried to make them feel inferior, the Dean went on sabbatical and canceled all our classes.

No conspiracy or theory was needed; I had all the evidence that proved our students tested well on the subjects of architecture, history, and environmental design. Submitting the evidence had no effect on the political decision by the Dean. We were never involved in a discussion regarding why we were no longer able to teach there, or given any warning of the Dean's decision.

The right to work for less, is determined by those at the top. We are told we can do nothing about this, because it is just 'the way things are'; so we should shut-up and stop asking foolish questions. To pursue the reasoning behind the assumption that 'state authority is necessary' to bully the population, is to commit career suicide. Only those in comedy are fit for that job.

Some of us will continue to do what we can, which is really the best we can do. I will stay involved in education, which for me means considering, questioning, and sharing knowledge. Even the homeless cynic Diogenes, wandered the streets with a lantern in search of an honest man; well he was not homeless really, since he had a large pot to live in.

There are some interesting cases of bonds between workers, which leads to unions and parties. Even in the military, bosses that hated me still knew they had to deal with me, and so there was often a respect for the power that I demanded be shared with me, and that was chiefly pay and self-defense. I let my bosses know, that if they pushed me hard, I could push back. I could have kept my military job, if my philosophy and ethics had permitted it; and I am proud of my service.

Crony capitalists remind me of car salesmen. They hang around in gangs with their business suits and ties, and from afar you can tell they are up to no good. We have to be able to laugh.

*

Futurist Science Fiction Propaganda

It may be worth imagining an interesting proposal by a future State Capitalist system for the newly disabled class, who are unable to find work:

"For those that cannot find a job, we have a new program to help make you disabled; then people might care for you better. We need to make sure you really will be crippled to the fullest extent, for you to qualify as unable to work for slave wages or find a job where the boss wants to keep you. Remember it is your duty to find a job, other-wise one WILL BE found for you under martial law in the military or prison system; which are the only two institutions that will take care of anyone that cannot or refuses to work within the capitalist system; unless they are disabled, in which case they can have whatever health-care their finances can afford. If they cannot afford to pay for help, then maybe if they end up homeless there will be some better support. There is a critical difference between those unable to work, and those willing to serve others. The only jobs available at this time, are health care-takers."

Fictional futuristic scenarios in popular films often have dystopian vs utopian themes and imagery. Some popular or 'cult' classics include: Blade-Runner, Running Man, Logan's Run, Total Recall, Matrix, and Judge Dredd,... to name a few. These films have ideas of society and freedom that resonate with many fans, and the deeper meanings do not elude the most interested.

Allow me to thank my conservative military masters. I am thankful that they allowed me to serve, and become a stronger warrior because of training and pay. I am very proud of my service and badges of courage, but am happier as a free artist.

*

I wonder if people think that poisoned water in Flint, Michigan and Charleston, WV are conspiracy theories? How many even heard those news stories, and then could get what that means politically? It was obvious that we need more people to hold corporations (incorporated towns and companies) accountable for the health and well-being of citizens. Controls on power are made with laws, or manifested within responsible family units sociologically, to make corporations respect that they cannot pollute our fundamental requirements for life to the level of killing us painfully or maiming us for life.

*

Slay the Hoarding Dragon!

The rich will be resistant to paying more taxes towards a more egalitarian system even in the future, just as any hoarder will be resistant to giving up their collections. Dragon slaying stories were originally in part about wealth distribution, as the greedy 'dragon' must be killed to win back the treasure of a land.

Saint George, Beowulf, and Sigurd were heroes that liberated innocent common people by slaying a single magical 'dragon' that had made the land to suffer under a terribly violent reign. The people lived in fear, under constant threat of violence by a local unique creature, whose very breath was toxic! Allegory was a traditional method of oral story telling, as is evident in far older mythologies, as well as the Bible.

Even the word 'dragon' itself has Pagan roots among many languages, regarding smoke and magic, medicine and control; but I will not go into that in this book.

The legend of 'Saint George and the Dragon' is one of the most famous and wide-spread tales of dragon slaying. When I went to Italy as a child, I became a fan of St. George paintings in galleries and common shops with St. George puppets and images. When I learned of the religious interpretation, I could no longer appreciate it as propaganda without any ethical reason, beyond the moral dogma stripped of original context. Now I think there was even more to the story.

According to the Golden Legend, the narrative episode of Saint George and the Dragon took place in Silene, Libya. In the Tenth-century Georgian narrative, the town was Lasia, and the idolatrous king who ruled was Selinus. The town had a small lake plagued by a dragon who poisoned the country. To appease the dragon, the people of Silene fed it two sheep every day. When they ran out of sheep they started feeding it their children, chosen by lottery. One time the lot fell on the king's daughter. The king, in his grief, told the people they could have all his gold and silver, and half of his kingdom, if his daughter were spared. The people spitefully refused, because they despised him. Citizens wanted the King to personally suffer emotionally like they did, by losing a loved one. The King's daughter was sent out to the lake, dressed as a bride, to be fed to the dragon.

George by chance rode past the lake. The princess tried to send him away, but he vowed to remain. The dragon emerged from the lake while they were conversing. Saint George made the 'sign of the Cross' and charged it on horseback, seriously wounding it with his lance. He then called to the princess to throw him her girdle, and he put it around the dragon's neck. When she did so, the dragon followed the girl like a meek beast on a leash. The princess and George led the dragon back to the city of Silene, where it terrified the populace. Saint George offered to kill the dragon if they consented to become Christians and be baptized. Thousands of men including King Selinus converted to Christianity.

George then killed the dragon with his sword, and the body was carted out of the city on four ox-carts. The king built a church to the Blessed Virgin and Saint George on the site where the dragon died. A healing spring flowed from its altar.

This ancient version resembles Greek mythologies of religious sacrifice to magical monsters by male leaders, with innocent female victims who are saved by a hero. Later Eleventh-century icons from Georgia show George slaying a human enemy rather than a dragon. The original motif became popular in Georgian, Russian, and Greek icons. The saint is depicted in the style of a Roman cavalryman (Thracian cataphract).

The motif of Saint George as a knight on horseback slaying the dragon first appears in more western countries like Italy and England in the 13th-century. The St. George's Cross coat-of-arms of red-on-white, developed after the crusades.

Rethinking the legends of Saint George and the Dragon makes me not only question the Christian interpretation of killing evil pagans, but also to wonder if originally it was a more important story of greedy despotic human leaders, whose victim population accepted sacrifice as 'the way things were', until a savor came and liberated them by slaying the 'dragon'. Early Christianity among common people was more concerned with the communal spirit of Jesus and his disciples, as a response to the wealthy elite that ruled them and caused artificial suffering by a rigged system to oppress and keep the tax or 'sacrifice' burden on the masses.

The power of the dragon (king) in the oldest versions was associated with the land's wealth, a hoard of treasure; just as Christianity was spreading it's communal spirit and threatening plutocratic authority. The idea of Pagan sin was clearly connected to the greed of wealth and politics, in contrast to the Christian purity and innocence of those without corrupt powers.

George the name means geos (earth), and orge (tilling). So George is to say 'tilling the earth', that is his flesh. And Saint Austin said in 'Libro de Trinitate' that "good earth is in the height of the mountains, in the temperance of the valleys, and in the plain of the fields". The first is good for herbs being green, the second to vines, and the third to wheat. Thus the blessed George was high in despising low things; he was tempered by discretion, gladness, and humility. He was a pilgrim, who suffered and was given sainthood by the crown of martyrdom. George's legend is numbered among other scriptures apocryphal in the council of Nicene. For in the calendar of Bede it is said that he suffered martyrdom in in the city of Diaspolin (Lidda), Persia. And in another place it is said that he suffered death under Diocletian and Maximian, which that time were emperors. He suffered death under Dacian the provost.

- Catholic Saints, Info (online domain)

Beowulf's Anglo-Saxon dragon and Sigurd's Norse dragon (origin of Siegfried's German dragon) were written in the Tenth-century, circa 1000 AD; but all seem to stem from the older mysterious Eastern-Roman (Third-century?) legend that evolved into 'Saint George & the Dragon'. The Germanic and Norse versions are worth considering also, in their earliest recorded forms. Those Pagan heroes were not Christian.

Sigurd was a legendary Viking hero who was included in Norse mythology. Sigurd was the central character in the Völsunga saga. His earliest legends come in pictorial form from seven rune-stones in Sweden and most notably the Ramsund carving (c. 1000) and the later Gök Rune-stone. The older origins echo real events in Central Europe during the 'Migration Period', chiefly the destruction of the Burgundian kingdom by the Huns in the Fifth-century.

Sigurd starts on a quest to avenge Regin and Hreidmar by killing Fafnir, who has been turned into a dragon by Andvari's cursed ring. Regin makes him a magic sword, Gram.

To kill Fafnir, Regin advises Sigurd to dig a pit, wait for Fafnir to walk over it, and then stab the dragon once he has fallen into the pit. Odin, posing as an old man, advises Sigurd to drain the dragon's blood, and bathe in the blood, for invulnerability. Sigurd follows the instructions given to him by both Regin and Odin and kills Fafnir. Regin then asks Sigurd to give him Fafnir's heart. Sigurd drinks some of Fafnir's blood and gains the ability to understand the language of birds. The birds advise him to kill Regin, since he was corrupted by the ring and is plotting Sigurd's death. Sigurd beheads Regin, roasts Fafnir's heart, and consumes part of it. This gives Sigurd wisdom (prophecy).

After defeating Fafnir, Sigurd meets Brynhildr, a shield-maiden. She pledges herself to him but also prophesies his doom and marriage to another. As Siegfried he is one of the heroes in the German 'Ring of the Nibelung', and Richard Wagner's operas. This of course brings us up to the present with Tolkien's books.

Tolkien loved Beowulf, a poem is set in Scandinavia. Beowulf, the hero, becomes the King of the Geats of Sweden. After a slave steals a golden cup from the lair of a dragon at Earnanæs, the dragon discovers the cup is missing, so it leaves its cave in rage, burning everything in sight. Beowulf and his warriors come to fight the dragon, but Beowulf tells his men that he will fight the dragon alone and they should wait on the barrow.

Beowulf descends to do battle with the dragon, but finds himself out-matched. His men flee in terror, and retreat into the woods; except Wiglaf, who comes to his aid. The two slay the dragon, but Beowulf is mortally wounded. After Beowulf's death, Beowulf is ritually burned on a great pyre in Geat-land; while his people wail and mourn him, fearing that without Beowulf, the Geats are defenseless against enemy tribes.

*

Sexonomics & Ecological Economics

The oldest profession might have been economics, as prostitutes needed a monetary exchange. The definition of 'selling one's self' was not bartering one service for another, but rather a more advanced notion of trading a service (sex) for currency, which represented future commodities. Combined with equipment and products, we now call that business (work trade).

Restructuring my conditioned capitalist brain to accept non-money payment in service to others, will take me years more retraining to not feel like a loser when I do things for free, pay huge sums to get less in return, and have minimal income. I feel I'm doing better than many men in worse situations, who will never accept the reality of their new place at the bottom of the economy. For a male ego, it may-be worse in some ways than for women, due to testosterone pride. I don't know. SCOD has a desire for social transformation towards a utopian system.

Everyone has bills to pay, but so many men depend on the bread-winner role for self-esteem. I've been trained to always be seeking to gain capital, by giving less and getting more; which sounds greedy, but is the basis of our system. You have to spend less than you make, to save or gain capital. It makes sense to try to be better people, a new type of wealth maybe; wealth of quality of life, which has more to do with psychology than with economics. The new way is more social, and less careless.

We need more wealth of spirit, in an agnostic way, but ethical with joy, enthusiasm, and motivational will-power that comes with liberty. Personal and social consciousness are considered important by many people. Laws, courts, and politicians always need to catch up with social evolution. Progressive leaders will always face opposition by most conservative leaders, even if the majority of the population supports their ideas.

Conventional economics is boring, but a New Green Deal is exciting. Ecological egalitarian economics is sexy, because it means more of us would be freer to pursue our sensible passions, travel, invent, explore, and experiment more with less health problems and less financial risk.

Democratic power systems are sapio-sexy, because more voting freedom energizes the population. We all get more enthusiastic in options that we feel we have some control of, concern for, or interest in. Being part of a larger system feels better when we feel that we can makes changes in it to benefit our ways of life.

An 'average' citizen was recorded saying that his interpretation of the DNC's take on the Hillary-email-Wikileaks-FBI scandal of the 2016 election, was as follows: Democratic politicians are telling us "If we were not caught lying about rigging the election in favor of Hillary, we would be running the country right now." A republican was quoted by the Washington Post saying "I think Putin pays Trump." These are global crony capitalist issues.

I am trying to be as gentle as I can in explaining the facts about corporate crony politics, I just cannot take time to debate theories all the time. The best I can do is to use my education to try to explain why things are the way they are, and provide choices for how to proceed into the future. I am not being paid much to do my work, and certainly not to fight opponents.

Fun fact: in 5th grade I published a gossip paper in my class, and sold copies. I wrote the paper less for the joy of gossip, which I consider frivolous and childish, but more for the attention of making a product and getting money for it. maybe I would be rich if I had pursued the tabloid profession, but my lack of respect and distaste for gossip (for the sake of gossip) made doing that as a career that impossible. My goals were always more political-economic, rather than sociological.

ECONOMIC Problems

Rich vs Poor is an economic class game that ignores national wealth inequality and the value of human life. Economic models show that if the richest 1% would NOT be allowed to hoard the nation's wealth, it would allow the poorest to be able to afford to live, and it would expand the middle class (Professor Mark Blyth, Brown University). Corporate profits are higher now than they ever were in recorded history (Robert Reich based on national statistics, accounting for inflation, since 1947, relative to percentage economy); Average Americans are not getting enough income to buy their products, so companies are buying their own stocks, like during the 1920s, you know.... just before the Stock Market Crash and Great Depression. The main argument against distributed wealth has always been war propaganda against Russia (Red Scare), which was really based on xenophobia, but it is American to believe we are 'all created equal' and 'we the people' get to decide in democracy.

In 2017 the Military Industrial Complex backed by our President is cutting funding for all humanitarian or ethical agencies, and pumping 50 billion more into the military. America spends over 600 Billion annually on the military budget, while all other countries spend under 200 billion, and most under 100-billion if they even have that much money (international economic budget statistics according to the IISS). The IISS is the International Institute for Strategic Studies; "a British research institute founded in 1958 for international affairs. Since 1997 its headquarters have been in London, England. The 2013 'Global Go To Think Tank Index' ranked IISS as the ninth-best think tank worldwide" (Wiki). We spend more on 'health care' than military, but half the country is poor, and can barely afford the basic costs of living including health insurance.

Our government does not work well for most of its population.

SCOD is developing an overall master plan for micro-economics between friends for communities, that can apply and be integrated with the larger existing economy, or an entire macro-economic synergy of SCOD amalgams. Surviving and thriving within our means should be our fundamental right to work in life. We should be allowed to survive by having our basic access needs met, in an organic environment aided by group systems, to be able to be self-sufficient; regardless of any desire for more wealth or other work. There will always be lazy and greedy people, but for the majority who are reasonable with the means to be rational, they can be who they are and do what they want without ruining a fair economic model for all.

We know that the SCOD economic model cannot be ruled by plutocrats, oligarchs, tyrants, or despots of any kind, even those claiming to be 'representatives'. Ancient Greece exposed the deadly flaws of democracy when they put Socrates to death, so there must be constant reminders of the worst human tendencies of mobs, and laws that respect civil rights that value life. This is the middle-ground between the existing patriarchal plutocracy dominated by aggression, and the future matriarchal or balanced utopia of an almost moneyless system based on right to life, right to work, and equal rights for 'We the People'. This means having natural renewable resources freely available for all.

People value what they want, but don't reach out to others who they don't think they want anything from. It is a natural problem that should be at least talked about more, as to how to value those that do not do what we want, or don't offer what we want, as many are not able to constantly adapt to what others want, because they recognize what they will be given in return is not always fair if they are generous and others are not. I think there is often a stalemate in these groups as to how to approach others. Differences in communication can cause huge problems when negotiating projects. If people can work out a friendly pattern of communication that works to solve complex problems before real tough issues come up, they should use all means necessary.

*

WEALTH

Ask a coal miner and a millionaire, "Which thinks they earned what they got, the most?" The problem of trying to earn a living working for poor people, is that they are POOR. SCOD thinks we need to use many approaches for fairer wealth distribution; time banks, shared projects, CSA's, Green Investments, time limits on holding money, etc.

In studying economic-futurist Michael Hudson's theories on Egyptian, Roman, medieval, renaissance, colonial, and modern economics; neo-feudalism is not sustainable"; post-industrial economy (de-industrialization) is replaced with finance capital, which means unemployment for you and lower wages for the few that work, due to robots, efficiency, and flooded markets. Productivity has gone up since the 1950s, but wages have tapered off, because the 1% rich have absorbed the wealth.

I'm listening to many economists who say that our economy we have now perpetuates the ruling rich. It is very interesting to find scod-type economists. They admit our systemic problem is that alternatives get black-listed by the establishment, to favor elites.

"Even Babylonian Kings canceled ALL citizen debts when they started a new dynasty. We have an Orwellian Double-Speak in politics today." "Things are worse than Piketty's conclusions. Paul Krugman does not admit that there are such things as economic rent, or unearned income. He is paid and given prizes to distort economic reality." - *Economist Michael Hudson*

Corporate politicians lie to the masses to maintain power.

Corporate politicians will continue lying to the population, to maintain power. They are bought by their supporters. It is not a fake theory, it is just reality. The people paying them to be in office, are not the masses, they are specific corporations who often are not even listed publicly. The money they get from campaigns and lobbyists and business friends is often more than their pay for the position. They serve their big business donors.

People have verbally attacked me publicly online and called me many rude names in messages regarding my research on understanding political economics. Funny none of my architecture designs based on the very same theories of sustainability vs market volatility do not attract as much hatred. I think that is because people have been conditioned to act in accordance with the 2-party system, and anything else they consider to be non-sense because it is not accepted in main-stream society. We are told to treat anyone that considers alternative theories to be 'tin-foil-hatters'; and even the word 'conspiracy theory' has been given a negative connotation with a false definition of 'something that is false or impossible'.

Bernie Sanders could become president with more actual Left-wing policies than any leader we have had since Franklin Roosevelt; without being forced into a war. Peace!!

I want to write an entire book about Education, but I will make some points about 'free national education'. When we use tax money in general for education, it is not flushing the money down the toilet like spending it on bombs. Educating a nation is an investment at every level of society, politics, and the economy. Smarter people contribute and benefit society so that we can work smarter if not harder, and it has been proven that thoughts can solve problems (see inventions).

On behalf of Libertarians I will mention that state, corporate, or religious propaganda in schools is also a real issue.

Many parents do not want their kids to be taught or conditioned about subjects or beliefs they oppose. To be fair to public education, it is impossible to please everyone. Perhaps using an organic village concept to raise children is better than putting the kid to work in a factory, office coup, or locking them in a closet. Civilization should realize how corporations are dividing us.

The problem of money in politics is so universally recognized that even Donald Trump, the ultimate capitalist, and Bernie Sanders, a self-described Democratic socialist, agree on it. Sanders has spent his career railing against the corrupting influence of wealthy and corporate donors, while Trump has unmasked the game by admitting that he gave money to politicians to curry favor with them. The success of both of these politicians suggests the degree to which Americans are fed up with the influence of money on politics. If we don't reduce that influence, our system risks losing its legitimacy.

"If Citizens United was so pivotal in aggravating the problem, the Supreme Court should overturn it. The ruling misinterpreted the First Amendment as a protection of money in politics, and it conflated corporations with individuals in a way that opened the floodgates for companies to spend millions—or even billions—to influence elections. If overturning Citizens United won't fix things, we should toughen up disclosure requirements so that at least people will know what individuals and organizations are paying for the ads they see on TV. We need to focus on empowering average people by reinvigorating and expanding the public-financing system for campaigns, both on the federal and local levels." - *the Atlantic magazine online*

Individual responsibilities are held within large systems of power; from gravity to government. People are forced into mortgage debt that benefits the banks, while making the buyer suffer unjustly. If housing was more affordable, people would be able to have more freedom in their lives and careers.

*

Money in Politics

"There is a growing disconnect between average citizens and elected officials. Part of the blame falls on a campaign finance system that unfairly stacks the deck in favor of the few Americans able to give exceptionally large contributions. Citizens United and other court rulings have obliterated decades of common-sense campaign finance laws. Now a handful of wealthy special interests dominate political funding, often through super PACs and shadowy nonprofits that conceal donors' identities from the public."

- Brennan Center for Justice at NYU School of Law

Political Finance

Political finance covers all funds that are raised and spent for political purposes. Such purposes include all political contests for citizen voting, election campaigns for public offices that are run by parties and candidates.

Modern democracies operate varieties of permanent party organizations. The Democratic National Committee (DNC) and the Republican National Committee (RNC) form our 2-party system in the US. The conservative RNC is run by neo-conservatives and the liberal DNC is run by neo-liberals; which means they are fundamentally corporate funded, so their political platforms often hide their sponsor motivations. In England they have the conservative Tory party for the rich and the progressive Labor party for workers, but similar things go on there like a mirror to the USA. In Europe the allied term 'party finance' is frequently used.

Political expenses can be caused by election campaigns, contests for nomination (or re-selection of parliamentary candidates), party training events, policy development, party operations, and propaganda education or data information.

Party headquarters spend on public relations, mass media, consultants, and offices. Local party chapters rely on volunteers (activists), cover communication charges as well as rent and utilities for storefront offices, which they use as their centers of political activity.

Political revenue may be collected from small donors and/or big donors. Small donors are individual citizens (grassroots fund-raising) who make small contributions or pay party membership dues. Big donors are wealthy individuals, companies, interest groups, organizations, and trade unions. Sources of funds are not only legal, but sometimes illegal. General illegal activities including graft; buying access, favor, offices, praise, extortion, or blackmail. Gidlund has classified the available options of fund-raising by three categories: member, plutocrat, and public.

Public grassroots fund-raising is having a revival. Popular government (vulgo democracy) should require that the people at large cover the costs of their democracy. Collection of small donations depends very much on the current mood of people's emotions towards politics, policies and politicians. A variety of ways are available (nationwide lotteries, direct mail drives, peer, neighborhood or internet solicitation, local social events) for grassroots fund-raising. Personal (door-to-door or peer group) solicitation was quite frequent in the fifties. Since the 1960s it has been superseded by telethons and computerized mass mailings. Recently internet solicitation has played a major role.

Plutocrat financing uses rich aristocrats, entrepreneurs, corporations, and super-PACs of the upper class. Super-PACs are 'political action committees' which raise unlimited sums of campaign money from corporations, unions, and individuals. Super-PACs are not supposed to coordinate directly with parties or candidates, but the vast amounts of money should raise criticism as serious evidence of bribery corruption.

Most modern democracies provide government subsidies for party activity, typically in finance and free access to public or private media. India and Switzerland are notable exceptions. Public subsidies can be relatively small (UK and USA) or quite generous (Sweden, Germany, Israel and Japan), and usually exist side-by-side with private fund-raising. Party organizations, parliamentary groups (party caucuses) and candidates are typically the recipients of public support.

Many countries have regulated the flow of political funds. Such regulation from the political finance regime, may include bans and limits on income, expenses, direct and indirect public subsidies, and transparency of political funds by disclosure and reporting. Reforms are made to adjust for changing problems.

Opensecrets.org has an online list of Lobbyist donor recipients for 2016. Listed at the top was Democrat Hillary Clinton with $2,084,162. Coming in second was Republican Van Hollen, at $540,041. Those amounts compete with their official office pay.

"Whether it is because Trump wants to impress a girl, to go to a summer home with Putin, I don't care... just as long as we don't start World WAR III!!!" - *Jimmy Dore*

Most 'bought politicians' seem fake, because they are not talented actors. It is the good actors that promise specific things we need to really pay attention to, and find out if they deliver their promises. If they don't deliver, their time is limited.

I signed **Impeach Trump Now** in 2017, by 'Free Speech for People' and 'Roots Action'; because threats that a worse tyrant may take their place without getting removed in turn, is not a reason to allow the current tyrant to remain in power.

*

Quest for Consciousness

Over the years I have toured many college campuses and made appointments to meet with staff members in their architecture departments. As friendly as some of the professors may have been, they told me candidly there were no job opportunities for me as part of their faculty, and of course none of them were paid to help me, and therefore they did not. I did lecture them on SCOD thesis, and they verified that college politics was not in my favor; despite 'sustainability' being a popular theory.

While exploring the Maryland University campus again in 2017 for open-house Maryland Day, among my various conversations, I did have a fortunate discussion with quantum physics graduate students and a business school professor, outside of the Science Department. We were talking about particle-wave theory, the split-test experiment, and the question of conscious observer, or whether turning the lights 'on or off' had anything to do with it.

I congratulated the business professor for being concerned about whether science could account for consciousness; as we have a cross-disciplinary problem of not being able to quantitatively value life-forms and the Eco-system in direct ways that protect our existence from predatory capitalism. He recognized that this problem did indeed exist, and that he "only went into business to make money", but he was very concerned about getting the scientific establishment to acknowledge that consciousness exists. I defended the students who had volunteered to answer public questions, by telling the business professor that he was "pushing the limits of their knowledge, because science is about conducting quantitative verifiable experiments; and I wish that spirit had a residue that we could measure (like ectoplasm), but there does not appear to be much evidence that conscious exists apart from biology." To ask whether Ghostbusters is real or not, is very amusing to me, and fun for the whole family.

Our two quests are linked, because monetary currency is mutually agreed upon around the globe, but life and environmental science are often ignored for profits that do not take their worth into account as variables that have economic value. If consciousness cannot be verified, given quantitative worth, and supported in monetary terms, then how can we ever develop Economic Consciousness for Life-forms? Perhaps we can begin with Bio-diversity preservation theories that do not depend on 'consciousness'. Climate Science is getting ignored currently also, so perhaps corrupt politics or predatory instincts are to blame. On a positive note, I went to the Art Department and explained this problem during another conversation about the value of art and artist income.

*

'To Star Trek Economics, From Our Present Point' - A SCOD Show Interview with Tom the Data Scientist; SCOD Talk on Economics. A discussion of how to forge economics towards a more utopian future like Star Trek (Federation Earth Planetary Government) - hosted by Drogo Empedocles.

I think we made a unique cutting edge science-fiction (scifi) contribution to economics, because both of us push the limits of what we think, in rare ways. Unlike paid program hosts, I actually take time to talk with interested individuals regardless of their pay-scale; but on a shoe-string budget quality is sacrificed. We dream that one day SCOD will have income.

Futurism depends on pushing and challenging visions, like a plot in a film like Bladerunner does. Only when we realize labels and terms change over time and are subject to propaganda on every side, can we fill the pages of our lives with more substantial content than even the best book cover can suggest. That is how scifi transcends time and place, it does not depend on only one way of pronouncing or defining words.

Even when a word meaning is agreed upon, the meaning of every word in the definition is subject to interpretation according to any number of perspectives, so communication is based on perceived intent of knowledge or control. Any communicator may be lying, wrong, or misunderstood in any number of ways. Understanding another person means consciously glimpsing what another person may think they mean, and then relying on recall of that glance.

*

Class Warfare

In 1729 Jonathan Swift wrote a 'Modest Proposal'. The anonymous essay "For preventing the Children of Poor People From being a Burden to Their Parents or Country, and For making them Beneficial to the Publick"; was a satire suggesting that poor Irish children be sold to rich aristocracy. It mocked apathetic, cruel, and bigoted British policies and popular opinions of the Irish.

The rock band Aerosmith released a song in 1994 called 'Eat The Rich'. As a punk rocker I listened to that song over and over, because it resonated with me as teen. Listening to it as an adult, the energized passionate satire is still very satisfying. I feel it is both evidence that I am still a punk, and also that the theme points out valid sentiments of class inequality.

Class warfare has always existed, and most of the battle strategies are perpetrated on the poor by the rich through economic policies. Some SCOD members are talking about a new tax idea that should be publicly considered - **Citizen Direct Allocation Taxation** (Tax Choice, Public Choice Theory). When a person pays taxes, they can allocate a portion directly to a government fund or budget of their choice.

*

FaceBook Annual Share-holder Meeting
Voted - April 25, 2017
Control #9605332137442159

I voted FOR all the share-holder proposals. To give you an idea of what they were about, all the Board Directors were against the proposals. Yes the proposals were for more equality and transparency, which can lead to more public information and user control, so that the FB application can function more like a democracy. We don't even get to vote on which Board of Director assholes we want dictating things, as stupid as they all may be; because they are all running un-opposed it appeared. so the best option was to "with-hold" all their votes.

If we don't have democratic structures able to function in society, I am for unionizing and co-opting corporations and turning them into entities that we can use better as groups of people (which is what corporations are supposed to be, 'incorporated corporeal bodies' of people). If it isn't possible to make improvements, all we would have left as leverage for rights is boycott, if at all possible under monopolies. Think WAYLAND Corp. and all the other dystopias, that may appear as utopias to consumers who have not seriously thought about alternatives. I do believe the co-opting of government by companies is a reflection of how corporations have been run, which has tended to be like banana-republics or the military (heavy on dictatorial top-down CEO power in the form of monetary reward for hierarchy and command decision authority). As many point out, it is traditional class plutocracy.

Realization of what the DNC did to Bernie Sanders in order to stop him from winning votes is a zeitgeist paradigm shifter. People can keep living in denial that the system is rigged against democracy, but when the crony corruption is clearly not in their favor, that catalyst knowledge leads to action against the establishment. Corporate Democrats do not deserve to be called democrats; they are representatives for corporations.

31

Service to others often has nothing to do with how much money is 'earned'. Just as how much money is 'earned' often has nothing to do with service to others. Fair compensation is rare when you consider common people that do the hardest jobs in society suffer and are given pitiful compensation compared to the money given to many rich people that will never have actually done as much service to others by physically harming their bodies like common laborers who are lucky if they are able to spend their savings on health care.

Fuck all those scrotum leeches that ever said "cut your hair and get a real job"! While that slogan has been common for generations, so has this one: "Take this job and shove it"! Assholes that put alternative people down are the jerks who were taught to bully others who are different. I know because I acknowledged that tendency inside myself long ago, and chose to pursue being a more loving person, instead of wanting to embarrass vulnerable people, leave them with less, or put others down to get ahead by being paid more, instead of others.

Those of us that object to needing to constantly sell ourselves as better than others to earn a living, don't fit within the system. We just want to be free to live our lives. Those main-stream people that attack us, deserve every bit of their dickish spite in return, twice as hard. The only way to break many bullies, is to do unto them what they do to others; until they believe there may be a more considerate and peaceful way to live with others.

It is common for people to have a subservient fear of upsetting authorities. We often say "Do not bite the hand that feeds you." My response to that is perhaps we should not be depending on authorities for food. "Let them eat cake."

"When the people shall have nothing more to eat, they will eat the rich." - *Jean-Jacques Rousseau 1700s*
*

32

"The first man who, having fenced in a piece of land, said 'This is mine', and found people naive enough to believe him, that man was the true founder of civil society. From how many crimes, wars, and murders, from how many horrors and misfortunes might not any one have saved mankind, by pulling up the stakes, or filling up the ditch, and crying to his fellows: Beware of listening to this impostor; you are undone if you once forget that the fruits of the earth belong to us all, and the earth itself to nobody." - *Rousseau 1754*

Not one ounce of the Earth belongs to anyone truly, not even the dust of their ashes. Temporary laws and opinions made by humans may claim 'property'; but that belief is at best temporary, and at worst a lie. Yes for a while we can agree that one thing is yours, and another is mine, but those are just jokes in the eyes of Time.

*

Progressive Banking & Micro-Lending
Esther Afua Ocloo (Nkulenu) was one of the founders of **Women's World Banking**, with Michaela Walsh and Ela Bhatt. To face down prejudice in Ghana against locally produced goods, she formed a manufacturers' association and helped organize the first 'Made-in-Ghana' goods exhibition in 1958. She was elected the first President of what became the 'Federation of Ghana Industries'. Esther was the first Ghanaian woman to be appointed as Executive Chairman of the National Food and Nutrition Board of Ghana. In the 1960s she moved into the tie and dye textile business. From the 1970s onwards Esther worked internationally for the economic empowerment of women. She was appointed as an adviser to the Council of Women, a member of Ghana's national Economic Advisory Committee, and Ghana State Council. Esther promoted the availability of credit for women to stimulate business, while she was a chairwoman of the Board of Directors of Women's World Banking into the 1980s. Esther received the 1990 African Prize for Leadership.

Green Children & Micro-Lending

'The Green Children' musicians Milla Sunde and Tom 'Marlow' Bevan, have a unique approach to pop music. They have helped to benefit the lives of some of the poorest people on the planet, by donating their time and money to micro-lending services.

They met Professor Yunus during their first trip to Bangladesh. They traveled there to see the amazing work of his Grameen Bank, and felt very fortunate to spend some time with him. They were inspired to work with such a rare but well-renowned humanitarian. He is a hero because he has amazing belief in the ability of people, and has succeeded where everyone said he would fail. He has dedicated himself to the potential of responsible investing, to gradually grow the middle-class by raising the poorest from poverty.

'Green Children' music royalties help to support a micro-lending Whole Planet Foundation project in India that was developed by Professor Yunus, which is related to his prize winning micro-finance Grameen Bank founded in Bangladesh. Poor people often do not have upper-class access to finance projects, due to lack of collateral. Micro-finance provides small loans to poor people so they can take the first step on the ladder away from poverty. It's about creating a long term solution, allowing people to take charge of their lives. Poor people can have ideas and ability, but they need opportunity. The repayment rate at Grameen Bank is 98% successful, and almost all the borrowers are women.

The name Grameen is derived from the word 'gram' which means "rural village" in the Bengali Language. Grameen Bank originated in 1976, as a project by Professor Muhammad Yunus at University of Chittagong, who studied how to design a credit delivery system to provide banking services to the rural poor.

Based on his project results, in 1983 the Grameen Bank was authorized by national legislation as an independent bank. In 2006, the bank and Yunus were jointly awarded the Nobel Peace Prize. In 1998 the Bank's "Low-cost Housing Program" won a World Habitat Award.

Muhammad Yunus earned a doctorate in economics from Vanderbilt University in America. He was inspired during the Bangladesh famine of 1974 to make a small loan of $27 to a group of 42 families as start-up money so that they could make items for sale, without the burdens of high interest under predatory lending. Yunus believed that making such loans available to a larger population could stimulate businesses and reduce the widespread rural poverty in Bangladesh. Grameen Bank is founded on the principle that loans are better than charity to interrupt poverty: they offer people the opportunity to take initiatives in business or agriculture, which provide earnings and enable them to pay off the debt. Grameen's objective has been to promote financial independence among the poor. Yunus encourages all borrowers to become savers, so that their local capital can be converted into new loans to others.

Some question the statistical validity of studies of micro-credit's effects on poverty, commenting on the complexity of debt and economic situations involved. Regardless of whether debt is better than donations, at least some poor people have some options on a civilized path towards a more equal World.

*

Eco-Villages

From the book 'Truth About Your Future, Money Guide':
"Ecovillages are for people concerned about the environment.
Named by the United Nations as one of the World's 100 Best
Practices for Sustainable Living in 1998, ecovillage residents
grow as much of their own food as possible, create homes using
local materials, operate renewable energy systems, protect
nature and safe-guard wilderness areas. Many communities even
create their own currencies, which helps them support each
other's small businesses. The Global Ecovillage Network lists
hundreds of ecovillages world-wide." The book also mentions
the National Association of Housing Cooperatives.

For more on eco-villages please visit the SCOD website and
blog, for more stories and links. Simply search 'SCOD villages'
and related terms, for links to environmental networks,
architecture, villages, and designs. Several American intentional
communities I have spent time at, have had various alternative
economic and ecological features; which I will collect and
explore for a later book called SCOD Eco-Villages.

SCOD Economics as a book can be applied to any type of ecovillage, or any amalgam of existing urban, sub-urban, and rural
developments. Houses, work-place offices, or mixed-use areas
or buildings all are affected by economics. Economics is an
artificial philosophy of exchange systems. We can focus on any
aspect of those systems that most interest us for their benefits or
problems. I believe we should use whatever methods 'work'.

*

Facebook, as much as any media bound by laws, plays a role in censoring society because so many people use it. Facebook (FB) has chosen to punish people on their own pages for artistic expression, while the company reaps profit from ads. FB is part of the authoritative narrative that maintains that female nipples are obscene, and all human bodies in their natural state should be shamed. Human genitals that are responsible for giving us LIFE itself, are banned; as FB encourages society to continue to consider our sacred parts rude, offensive, and inappropriate for public knowledge or art. Pagan art celebrates nudity in society.

The women of Pussy Riot and Femen are protesting in Europe more shockingly than in America, ironically because they have less freedom and less legal rights. Women in America have become complacent because they have largely bought into the commercial corporate male model of society. Those European martyrs are exposing their vulnerable bodies, shouting with their fragile voices, and putting their spirits in danger because we live in authoritarian state-run societies. Societies (as a whole) in Civilization evolve as cultures change through-out Time, and are influenced by those willing to defy traditions or conventions; often at the expense of their own safety.

Drogo's Diaspora Blog Bio
I am an Artist, Author, and Architect from the metropolitan DC area, USA. I have worked many jobs, but SCOD (The Sustainable Cooperative for Organic Development) is my life's work and self-employed career path. SCOD is a non-profit organization for organic design World-wide, in all areas of study. I am most interested in art and writing. I believe in Organic Education, meaning the freedom for anyone to pursue self-education and participating in the ongoing history of Civilization. [#nsfw tag = "Not Safe For Work"]

*

Making Movies

In my teens I had some experience co-founding and running an anarchist syndicate for a few years. Our group was called 'Death-To-Tourists-Entertainment!'. We did not make money, we made comedy movies and skits. We were only able to pull off our disestablishmentarianism because our servants slaved all day at jobs so they could feed, clothe, and shelter us even when we didn't work. Our only way of surviving in an insane world was to form an anarchist collective, and create products ourselves for ourselves as human beings without money. In only a few years we made several films and dozens of sketches. It became clear to me that our parents were suckers.

Getting Mugged

I was mugged in college, walking the sidewalks of Savannah, Georgia. My Muslim friend of mine and I were returning some library books just after dark, and two black guys on a bicycle rolled up behind us. They began talking to my Muslim friend, so he stopped. I kept walking, because every day in that city I was asked for money, but I did not usually have any money to give; so I would usually politely greet them or try to ignore them if I had to get some where and didn't feel like getting into a conversation, which sometimes happened. One of the young black men chased after me, and threatened to shoot me if I kept walking. I stopped and turned to see he was hooded, and his hand was reaching around his back waistline as if for a gun. I threw down my library books, and told him he could fight me, but I don't have any money. We had a stand-off. After a few moments of staring at each-other's eyes for a first move, I looked back towards the other two men. I did not see the punch coming, but he knocked me back, and cut my eye open with something sharp that was in his hand. As our two muggers escaped on their bicycle, I called after them to come back and fight. Since we were on foot, and I was wounded, we went to the Library and reported the mugging to the security guard there.

Later that night, as I was at our anarchist headquarters (shared apartment with communal chores on Park Avenue), the cops took me to go identify two young men that fit our description they had picked up. In the following days my Muslim friend became so scared that he fled the USA back this the middle-east (ironically). I testified alone at the court hearing. The old judge seemed to be asleep most of the proceeding. I was confident that those were the men that mugged us, and the guy that hit me had an aggressive response and look in his eye that I recognized and felt verified my memory. His mother begged me in the hallway to drop charges, but I told her it was out of my hands and for the public good, regardless of how hard she tried to be a good mother. The teen that mugged me had been from NY City, and ended up doing some time behind bars.

*

Predatory Commercial Corporate Capitalism

We are in a period akin to the 1920s, when 'The Great Gatsby' written, and the Coal Mine Wars happened. That period created Nazis in Germany, who used the allure of Fascist wealth to trick poor voters. The stock-market was booming for a few rich, and the masses who did not get significant wage increases were told to buy stocks, because the banks were not paying interest to savings accounts. Then the stock market crash, the Great Depression, and WW2 forced change. Perhaps like the 1930s book Brave New World, we are headed for a Gattica future.

In redneck states Boone and Crockett legends taught us many of our morals. Those two pioneers were not company industrialists, and preferred individual independent natural freedoms. The 2-party game acts like coal companies to keep workers divided, at each-others' throats. No WV hero ever said we should be lackeys or toadies to plutocrats.

A corporate democrat visited my small town to film a campaign commercial at our Methodist church. I was a registered independent by then, as I had founded my college thesis (SCOD) on how corporations had corrupted our system for their benefit and our loss. I still prefer most democrats to republicans, and if we are forced to live within the system as population grows, then social programs are the way to go. So I gave the candidate a chance to explain his policies, while we all sat like a loyal audience silently. Instead of explaining to us what he believed in, it became clear that he was an actor in a commercial for a health-care company. After several takes ordered by the commercial director telling us when to clap, I stood up and shouted that this political mockery was not democracy, and I left. No one followed me out. That game continues today.

We do need more grassroots activism in all parties and places. Some will want to join the big parties, others like me will prefer smaller parties. Yes primaries matter, and some people can play that game for me, while I represent more progressive voters that are not considered in an unfair 2-party system, just to remind people that other opinions should be allowed in democracy. We should all be able to vote for who we want, not the least corrupt of two clearly corrupt candidates who sold out. I admit I have been tricked into voting for main-stream candidates, which was basically like wasting my vote. However I can only vote based on my own wisdom at the time, so if a popular 2-party candidate sells me on their convictions, I reserve the right to vote for them.

Full-employment economic theory has an ongoing battle inherent in the system: Demand-side (workers contribute) vs Supply-side (workers compete). Trickle-down economics plutocracy style is supply-side theory of control. Free-market economics libertarian style would be demand-side.

*

As I listen to an old Frank Lloyd Wright (FLW) voice recording, I remember how learning his theories in high school set me on my path. In the recording, FLW says architects today have no formal way to get the organic design education he advocates; and that was 1950s. Remember the International business community thought Mussolini was good for Italy, because the trains ran on time. "I am not a number", "I am not a robot", "I am not a slave"; these quotes are related to our reality.

Around the world, people fight because of greed. In Africa and Asia they are chopping up bodies every day. Those continents revolve around the US Economy and Military. West African Cameroon has a long-term Dictator Paul Biya, and because of greed, and the power of Boko Harum, the people are cutting each-other to pieces, literally. The people of that country are shooting and chopping up their bodies. I only know this because my friend Njang Lionel told me. Lionel is from there and experiences the horrors and the media blackout. Lionel says that Nigeria and Cameroon are in hell because of Boko Harum. War for resources is pitting English Christian Africans against French Muslim Africans. Lionel also travels to South African Swaziland, and is lucky to have a good family business.

The mystery of private detectives is that they were historically thugs for Companies. I did not understand this as a kid, I thought they were like Sherlock Holmes, or the Radio Show cartoons, just waiting to help citizens and police to solve crimes.

SCOD PANANIMUS - In the Tri-State Area

How do we get from our present to a Star Trek future? We talk about Economics, Government, Environmental Ethics, Civil Rights Morality, Science & Technology in 2017.

"Our economic system doesn't allow anyone to become more than 5x richer than average. We don't have omnipotent financiers or industrial dictators." - *Pala Island, by Aldous Huxley*

41

When we sell-out or destroy natural wilderness, we console our-selves by saying it is the way of 'progress', and "If I didn't do it, someone else would."; a reference to Aldous Huxley's book Island. We have a tendency to ignore the wisdom of Dr. Seuss' Lorax; "UNLESS someone like you cares a whole awful lot, nothing is going to get better. It's not."

Conspiracies happen, and have happened throughout history. People are often shocked about the idea that people hold meetings to make plans in private (secret) all the time; we can admit that it happens, and it is a real thing. In government 'profit motive' becomes a big deal, and we need to learn how to govern ourselves better. Theater and Politics are very related.

*

HG WELLS, HUXLEY, & ORWELL

One similarity between Brave New World and 1984 is that both futures believe that "History is bunk", and the controllers constantly erase even yesterday's news, while using confusing hypocritical propaganda. Brave New World being more Left-wing, and 1984 being more Right-wing. Trump seems to have a regime that believes in this idea of Double-speak, according to the changes going on in all departments. Huxley wrote critical satire of HG Wells' utopian books; and contrasted his own writings to Orwell's 1984.

HG Wells wrote a few Utopian 'science fantasy' novels; set in 'parallel worlds' using concepts of democratic socialism, inspired by the Fabian Society. HG Wells wrote: Anticipations (1901 non-fiction); Mankind in the Making (1903 New Republic non-fiction); 'A Modern Utopia' (1905 fiction), 'Men Like Gods' (1923 fiction).

'A Modern Utopia' (1905) - [Parallel World named Utopia] - a voluntary order of nobility known as the Samurai could effectively rule a "kinetic and not static" world state so as to solve "the problem of combining progress with political stability." , vegetarian ascetic Rule ; mandatory annual one-week solitary ramble in the wilderness ; social theory of Utopia, four "main classes of mind": The Poietic, the Kinetic, the Dull, and the Base ; Economics - The world shares the same language, coinage, customs, and laws, and freedom of movement is general. Some personal property is allowed, but "all natural sources of force, and indeed all strictly natural products" are "inalienably vested in the local authorities" occupying "areas as large sometimes as half England." The World State is "the sole landowner of the earth." Units of currency are based on units of energy, so that "employment would constantly shift into the areas where energy was cheap." Humanity has been almost entirely liberated from the need for physical labor: "There appears to be no limit to the invasion of life by the machine."

'Men Like Gods' (1923) - [Parallel World named Utopia] "Our education is our government," a Utopian named Lion says (men like gods 1923), set apx. 3,000 years in our technological future on a parallel world ; Several characters in the novel are directly taken from the politics of the 1920s. Rupert Catskill probably represents Winston Churchill, as he was seen at that time: a reckless adventurer. Catskill is depicted as a reactionary ideologue, criticizes Utopia for its apparent decadence, and leads the attempted conquest of Utopia. ; Earthlings are quarantined on a rocky crag after infections they have brought cause a brief epidemic in Utopia. There they begin to plot the conquest of Utopia, despite Mr. Barnstaple's protests. He betrays them when his fellows try to take two Utopians hostage, forcing Mr. Barnstaple to escape execution for treason by fleeing perilously. Life in Utopia is governed by "the Five Principles of Liberty," which are privacy, free movement, unlimited knowledge, truthfulness and free discussion (allowing criticism).

There is Hope.
Tulsi Gabbard proposed a bill to legalize Weed.
Immigrants are speaking out against corporations that exploit.

From a scientific and capitalist point of view, life has no quantitative value; we are subject to being devalued as a default by monopolies. This ethical problem does upset me emotionally, due to cognitive dissonance. Consciousness is worth talking about. Threats to ife are disturbing. Working for pay (regardless of how ethical the work) has led to mercenary state authorized atrocities through-out history. Some say Life is priceless.

*

I Traded My Tracker for a Prius in 2017
Sold Tracker for $500, bought Prius for $7,000
2009 Prius Body Style: 5dr Model#: 1220
Fuel / Engine: 1.5L I4 SMPI DOHC
Mileage: 153,639
VIN: JTDKB20U197838155
Ext. Color: Blue / Passengers: 5
Gas Miles-per-gallon: 48 CTY / 45 HWY

The Prius was newer than my Tracker, but had more mileage. However when I add up the long term savings, and safer features for urban driving, the investment seemed worth spending a few thousand on. Both cars are reliable, but they still make Prius parts. Hard tops are safer and warmer in the Winter.

*

Owning Property

Amongst families, ownership claims of people and property
have intense power dynamics that can last many years.

My father had a secure full-time job that paid well and was worth doing. However he did not get along with many of his coworkers, so he would often come home and verbally take out his frustrations on me and Mom. Jealous that we spent peaceful playful time at home, often led him to start yelling when he came in the door, to aggressively announce to his large house (that he bought) that he was home and wanted to complain about work and Mom, by name-calling like he was taught in the military. I learned that if I was silent, they would play out a 'fight fire with fire' scenario for hours; but as I got older if I started defending Mom and yelling at Dad, then he would be forced to back down sooner. After a few hours, things would settle down and we could have dinner, and Dad would apologize. This would happen most weeks of my life growing up, but to be fair we also had fun good days too. My parents loved to remind me that they 'owned the house' and therefore even though they loved me and wanted me to contribute, they could always argue and deny me any rights based on ownership.

Ironically Mom controlled our family finances (his paycheck), paid all the bills, balanced the check-books, and earned her own significant income at various arts & crafts jobs. I will not go into more detail here, to respect my parents, and because I have heard many worse stories from friends about abuse in their families. This often happens in families where the adult off-spring fails to gain enough capital to buy their own castle, regardless of fault, and so transition of power never occurs, even after the death of parents who don't believe in inheritance or never planned, but still wanted ownership over all their property and offspring, so long as they lived there in that place.

While having money can help alleviate stress because we need it to pay bills, it does not solve problems of abuse that stem from psychologies of jealousy, ownership, and raw anger that pervade society. In some cases the drive to make money and possess can make things worse for everyone. I have lived through such scenarios, and I am in part a product of these problems, and a survivor that refuses to be caught in the pattern trap. When I fight others now, I want it to be for a good purpose or cause; because I am a fighter, and sometimes we need to fight against problems in various ways; rather than always accept the 'way things are' (apathy). Realistically accepting the way things are, does not always have to lead to lazy and irresponsible apathy, but can allow us to directly address serious problems, because we do know what our reality is and we want some real change.

Chelsea Manning's reason for leaking classified information, was to reveal that we had illegal torture policies and practices during a war for profit based on false pretenses. Our 2-party government's response was to imprison and torture Manning for years while the criminal war of terror continued. So clearly working for rich contract companies does not solve abuse or further world peace.

*

Corporate Chemical POISONS

First rule regarding Corporate POISONS: #1 DO NOT TRUST THE COMPANY; Second rule regarding Corporate POISONS (and big money influence): #2: Do not trust the 'test results'.

My grandfather was poisoned by arsenic lead that the company said was safe for farmers to breathe in the fields. It made his lungs bleed because it actually did poison him, despite their claims. Any chemical manufactured and sold commercially should not be trusted to be 'safe', even if 'scientists tested it'. The only chemicals we can truly ever trust, are natural organic chemicals that humans have worked with for hundreds or better yet thousands of years. Poisons can have negative affects on some carbon-based life-form species who have DNA; because Ecology and Biology have sensitive synergetic systems.

"More than 50 agricultural workers southwest of Bakersfield, California in Kern County were inadvertently exposed to pesticide drift from a nearby field earlier this month. According to local reports, 12 farm-workers reported symptoms of vomiting, nausea and one person fainted due to exposure to Vulcan, an organo-phosphate-based chemical. Notably, the active ingredient in the insecticide is chlorpyrifos, which the U.S. Environmental Protection Agency (EPA) under Trump decided not to ban in March." - *Ecowatch magazine*

*

Corporate Media Fails Democracy

Sadly it is up to bloggers and independent media to hold corporate government and media accountable, as underfunded as we are. In 2016 I would watch Bernie Sanders lectures online with enormous live crowds, while all news networks ignored his popularity; and instead chose to air Clinton and Trump as their two preselected favorites. This media bias occurred every single day, every week, for months during the National election campaigns. It was blatantly obvious to me time after time, that our public news was being filtered in favor of the two candidates that their bosses had decided were worth reporting on. It was a ridiculous 'good guy vs bad guy' show, with no room for rational public dialog on issues that affect us.

The failing of big news media outlets to cover all the candidates was not just by 'for-profit' corporations like the major commercial TV networks, but also newspapers and 'non-profits'. Obviously commercial news networks [FOX, NBC, ABC, CBS, CNN, Washington Post, NY Times] would not want to advocate any politicians that threaten their corporate sponsors, but apparently even the 'liberal' news shows of NPR & PBS were not immune to their corporate sponsors either, despite receiving our tax payer money (some government funding) and a majority of their money from PUBLIC pledge-drives!! I will no longer donate to my beloved NPR or PBS until they begin to cover the smaller candidates much more during (at least) National elections. Usually NPR or PBS were the only intelligently sensitive news sources I had to rely on for many years, and I still love many of their shows. However the National election press coverage clearly showed that corporate money corrupts even the media, not just our government. In hind-sight they have done this with many other 'lesser known' but brilliant candidates that have represented popular beliefs, like Dennis Kucinich, Mike Gravel, and Cynthia McKinney.

We must remember that our media and government is there to serve us, not the other way around. If corporations insist on forcing us to submit to their influence, by dictating what or who gets propaganda and attention and how they get it, then we must not only resist but supply alternative solutions and vote for change. We the people must unite and show our opinions for support or boycott publicly. Thank you to all those who have done this resistance fighting already!!! Remember, remember, how they foiled our democracy; and have been doing it for a long time. Please continue to seek the truth so that democracy can work for us. We must all become citizen journalists.

*

Faerie homes as models for human SCOD houses, is a fun idea! Bird houses can be models for human tree houses. Mushroom huts can be used by ground critters, using natural materials mostly, and allowing them to stay outside for animals or insects to use. Some experiments have been conducted, results vary.

*

New stories will be written of Renewable Energy and Green Economy amalgams, where stewards and custodians take pride in their work. No longer will we be raping the earth and treating people as slaves to corporations, but we will be preserving the future for generations of innocents. Scandinavians and small countries are already doing it, more than America has yet.

Iceland jailed its corrupt corporate crony politicians, Finland pays its citizens a 'universal wage for living', Denmark, Norway, Sweden, and others are using solar, wind, geothermal, and hydro power for public buildings and utilities funded by those that can afford to share and provide for the people of their countries. Even Germany, with its terrible recent political past, home to the most evil government of modern times (Nazi), is way ahead of America in Green Technology and ethical environmental policy.

SCOD Designs

SCOD vehicle designs: leaf mobiles, acorn saucers, bubble machines, rainbow riders, moss crawlers, branch swingers, cloud makers, puddle boats, plasma rollers that fit in plasma domes.

SCOD Eco-villages: Bio-diverse communities that design, build, inhabit, maintain, and develop environmental architecture and ways of life; Eco-villages fit into SCOD Amalgams. SCOD Amalgams: combination collages of SCOD Ecovillage master plans, designed for manifesting in phases over time; Amalgams fit into SCOD Matrix. SCOD Matrix: Total SCOD Master Plan; includes our literature, art, and amalgams. Land is vital so the organic nature of sites is preserved in urban Amalgams for higher population to green space ratio. Hives act as county council and ecology centers. Rural Amalgams low population to green space ratio, Eco-villages surrounded by wilderness.

SCOD designs often must modify existing architecture, in order to serve the new ecological-collective networks which extend into various communities. Homesteads become Nature Centers, which preserve the natural environment for maximum acres of hunting and gathering, with minimal impact housing and trading. Economics becomes subservient to Government based on environmental stewardship for harmonious cohabitation with renewable energy resources.

*

Trump sees himself like President Andrew Jackson.
There is so much essay material there.

*

Laughing is important!
"I am not the worst at being the best." - *Aeyla*

The most typical critic just says they don't like your work, and then you either have to beg them to explain, or try to take whatever you want from their opinion, and try to ignore the negativity and move on. This is not always easy to maintain for many artists, as not all of us always have the patience or desire to be respectful no matter what others say or do; nor do I think that maturity has no limits, or that we all should try to be what others might consider gentle, with what we consider rude.

Balance in work, eating, drinking, and play is good. Pacing and Moderation in all things, the pendulum swings. Sometimes pushing the limits, sometimes diminishing and centering. Attempting balance is a challenge, as forces can push too much in one direction, other forces can bring things back around, past the middle, and in the other direction.

Health Care Talk with Aeyla of the Hill People
"My doc of over 15 years just charged me $300 as a new patient because I hadn't been to see them in over 18 months. I called to complain, but Viking isn't returning or answering my calls. It's bad that I'm being punished for being healthy. He saw me for 5 minutes, none of my insurance info or anything else had changed, then he gave me drugs that made me want to puke for 2 weeks, then I ended up finding an herbal supplement that has almost cured my ailment in 30 days. I started taking willow bark for my tendonitis, instead of the Celebrex he prescribed."

*

About my friend Rhonda Selesnow

Rhonda Vision is an American Phenomenon. She idealizes a classic American feminine beauty that is easy to love for several reasons. Besides being talented and creative, she is a natural actress, which means her true personality is expressed in roles. With Rhonda her art tends to be full of complexity and passion. Her humor often comes in the form of post-modern satire and paradoxical contradictions. She clearly lives to perform comedy and entertain others. Rhonda intuitively understood at a young age what Democritus and Shakespeare wrote about concerning Life, the World, and Theater.

ART & Literature DRAMA

Writing is connected to acting. The line between fact and fiction and life, in books, and in performances it gets blurry. Drama shows us our mental relationship with reality. music, art, and drama evoke feelings that can be very conflicting; because it evokes the psychological issues we have, whereby the human mental neocortical process judges ourselves and everything else based on perceptions of senses and emotions. audiences are crying out to have the freedom to pass through the veil and explore between the worlds of art & reality. Most people are confined to a life where they are told acting is not authentic, art is not real, and so they rarely dare to go outside the confines of slave-wage jobs that pay the bills. The art of acting remains a mirror world to them, that they don't view as participatory; because they see it as an illusion to criticize. Obsessive fans are up against the mirror, touching the surface. The best artists are actors that reach through the mirror from the other side, and pull in those that want to cross the line. Democritus and Shakespeare wrote similar ideas concerning Life, the World, and Theater.

*

The 'Velocity of Money' bottoms-up!

The 'freedom vs slavery' tug-of-war ideology is ongoing as part of civilization. Leaders will always try to pull people to do things, and benefit from their efforts; meanwhile people want to benefit too, but when they realize they are not being paid fairly compared to the leaders, they will insist on getting a better share. Sometimes the emphasis becomes about Poor vs Rich, or Peace vs War, or Civil Rights vs Martial Law; but this inner dynamic of civilization is always about populations taking the liberty to resist or break their servitude to elite bosses, in order to better the lives of individuals in groups whose collective conscious evolves over time.

Scientists may be influenced by Corporate Oil agenda funding for projects. To what extent are scientists influenced by Corporate Oil agendas, when they receive funding for projects? How does it affect scientific studies for renewable energy or climate studies? Scientists pride themselves on independent thinking, but in a world where even taste in clothing is peer reviewed, and our Gangster President puts Oil Company men in charge, how much does political social pressure play (even if blatant bribery is taboo)?

The National Defense Authorization Act (SECTION 10-21 of NDAA) ignores Habias Corpus; which means anyone can be jailed without trial if authorities claim the accused are 'terrorists'. The judge ruled it Un-Consitutional, so a hold was put on it, which was just overturned. Similar to how the FBI treated MLK and others. The United States government considered Nelson Mandela a terrorist until 2008. - *ACLU article*

I first learned American History formally in 9th Grade from a veteran Marine, Mr. Lewis.

*

Creative Work

It is impossible to know which people will like what, when I make a work of art. For me, I make what I want to create or provide for others, and if at least one other person values what I do enough to help me to live and keep creating, then I am as successful as I can be, on my own terms.

I can believe that my work is good using self-esteem, but experience has taught me humility with gambling on predictions that involve the 'fickle' human. If I have spent hours working on a project, of course I would like it to be valued by others, and at the very least my friends. However, in a society that places monetary value on some products that seem to have no quality, while neglecting most human lives as 'worthless', I can say with conviction that I do not know what I can make, that some one else cannot make better or cheaper in their own way. Who am I to say that they should not desire their own work or the work of someone else over mine? I am me, and all I can do is what I am able to do.

SCOD News Updates - SNU

Total News Satire, SNU is Social Commentary through Comedy. Covers: Home, National, International, Solar System, Universal. "Allow me to say some stupid things, and adjust my tie. Thanks for listening, and remember to keep consuming commercial products and polluting. Have you met your daily national pollution quota? Remember, this is not a democracy."

As corporations control the media, it is vital WE BECOME THE MEDIA as much as we can. Listen, learn, investigate, share with others as much as you can; even if you are a not into boring news, you can make information that affects us interesting and creative. It is the only way to hold politicians accountable, as Trump fires attorneys and press. Feminism is important because men have been raping people and the planet a bit too much.

I love my SNU series because it is a combination of some of my favorite shows: Twilight Zone, SNL Weekend Updates, Daily Show, Colbert Report, and many other comedy, music, and sci-fi ideas. Most importantly I care about it because it allows me to express my deep frustration with many problems that we face in society and civilization as a whole. I can press the 'pedal-to-the-metal' with my punk rock commentary, using dark satire and sick jokes. I leave it to true hippies to make only uplifting happy shows that don't hit hard and prefer to tip-toe on egg-shells.

SNU News Anchors: Dr. Robot Shit-for-brains, No One, Mr. Nono, Speedy the Hyperactive Hypochondriac; Star Trek Theme music; Three Series Episodes: during March, 2017

*

Although I did not take college classes on Economics, I did stidy Structural Math and Physics. I was forced to do higher math for architecture. Then with my military training as a civil engineer, I had to use a translator during the torture interrogations.

ASD Allowable Stress Design : $1/0x0/1=(1+1/0)(1/0)$

Load and Resistance Factor Design LRFD = USD ? Strength Design

Gravity Force = GmM/d^2 ; Gravitational Constant (G) = 6.67×10^{-11} (N) x m^2/kg^2 ; m = mass1 ; M= mass2 ; d= distance;

Sphere Volume: $(Pi/6)D^3$

Accoustics: Multiple Sources of Sound : iL = 10 log i/io

io = 10^{-16} ; iL=sound intensity level in decibels

*

We are truly pioneers in a brave new age, of global communication between international citizens.

CIA Wikileaks Vault 7: Our CIA wants to be able control more and more whenever they want for undetectable covert actions. They can already listen in with any of our digital devices. We are told that it is not possible yet to remote control common cars, because the driving system is separate from the electronics that are remote controlled. Knowing is half the battle. An informed public is necessary for democracy, it is not just paranoia to understand our reality and debunk those that want to label everything as 'conspiracy theory'. To think that secret agencies set up to protect the public, would not conduct plans to hurt members of the public, does not take into account the history that they have certainly made plans to do so in official documents: Project Northwoods, Project MK-Ultra, and a few others that we now have on public record.

All we can do as peaceful citizens is to be aware, talk about what needs to happen, and vote for candidates that seek to actually create government transparency at the highest levels, and help pass protections that reduce state sponsored terrorism, and fund workers as a human right, in the ways that wise humanitarian leaders would.

History is recording the events of politics in more ways than ever. I have a feeling as long as average people are documenting their stories, our future leaders will be held to their service by millions of multifaceted accounts. No leader will be able to deny crimes against humanity as easily as in the past. Digital writing, images, and recordings are starting to educate and inform the masses of democracy; in ways undreamt of by our founding fathers. Yes misinformation and propaganda is a problem in commercial society, but overall the volume of tools and people around the world to learn from is overwhelming.

*

Meteor Threats

We had a few small asteroids pass Earth recently, they came very close and were hard to detect because they were small. The next near Earth asteroid will make its closest approach on October 26th, 2028. The asteroid's path is predicted to pass beyond the Moon's distance from the Earth. In fact, it will still be about two and half times farther away from the Earth than the Moon. It measures a mile-wide and is traveling at a speed of 30-thousand miles per hour. If it did strike New York City, the force would flatten everything from D.C. to Boston. It is not predicted to cause any problems.

Natural disasters like meteors, floods, hurricanes, earthquakes, tornadoes, and small local events do happen; which can deplete anyone's finances or kill them. Drive safe, drive slow; unless an avalanche is coming, then speed up! Another definition of 'economy' means efficiency.

*

SCOD is preparing a grant application with Lush cosmetics. We are currently care-taking with local poor who also need health care, but have not gotten financial aid for disabilities. Helping disabled people to function in society, can mean helping artists and writers with no income to write and publish books. SCOD works with illustrations and photography, to document the existing conditions of poverty and folk crafts. We also educate low-income people about economics and ecology. We deliver aid to those in need, helping dreams come true to bring hope to those with severe illness.

*

Open Letter to the National Security Agency

"Dear NSA, I hope you are listening because I heard a really cool plan to kidnap a gaggle of corporate politicians. Someone said that the CIA had a plan to put bags over the heads of the all most ignorant trumpsters, throw them in a van, and take them to a secure secret location... you know the one. Then those idiots will be forced to watch nature documentaries for many days while being told they are loved by a Pagan Goddess. Finally after they are starving and broken, they will be released naked into the wild. I can't tell you who I heard this conspiracy from, because then I would have to spank you (plus I cannot recall as Reagan and every politician says that is ever put on trial for war crimes). The FBI already threatened to blackmail and torture me, but they are just jealous of the CIA. Please try your hardest to monitor any communications about this plot, as I am very worried that someone's feelings might be hurt. I suggest spending millions of dollars of taxes from the poor and middle-class, like you normally do. Love, Bright Bard" - *from a new fiction book, Trumpster Gate: A Conspiracy Theory*

*

Progress has allowed us to live with more freedoms and free time, if national wealth is shared fairly. There are economic models which imply that our goals for less people to work as hard, and to combine play and work, can be realized if governments make laws that fit that economy. With the internet and cell phones, we have more means to use democracy. Anyone that wants more than the basic right to live, can work harder or smarter than others. Don't take the basics away from others. Future generations could come to view what we consider 'utopian' to be common sense, so long as democracy flourishes by keeping tyrants away from power. That will take more work as citizens than we have been spending towards those goals. Taking away all the humanitarian agencies of government, and denying progressive ways of earning income, as Trump's corporate cronies do, is unsustainable policy for the masses.

It is hard to get much attention for philosophy, books, or anything; markets are flooded for average people with no significant income streams, regardless of any advertising. Corporate politicians have declared war on education, middle class, poor, and the environment. My family has been dedicated to education, the NPS, and the EPA for many years. If you defend Corporate Politicians who are now taking away everything we hold dear, we are not going to get along. It is hard to see things from the perspective of people who are now taking away everything we hold dear. They know goddamn well, corporate political theory is not about humanitarianism or environmentalism, it is about profits for owners despite natural workers' rights. False advertising tries to convince us they care. In many ways Trump political theory is worse than Anarchy, because it wants to create chaos to secure Fascism. For some reason we cannot use a direct vote (it means a real vote) to choose our president, and cannot have debates on real issues, in an age where we are putting microchips in pets; and all of recent close elections keep getting nudged to the republican candidates, despite the popular votes.

Dear plutocrats, environmental pollution is real, it actually happens. Causing and perpetuating WAR does not help. Keeping the masses economically and intellectually impotent so we give you all our wealth in corporate machines so only rich elites get to decide everything, is not democracy. People power is unionizing the World, not just the Nation, so go green or give up. Limits on power is a good thing for everyone. - *Valentine*

FBI is our Mom and CIA is our Dad, playing us. They tell us Capitalism & War are Christmas & Santa Claus, by distracting us with song and dance. In Iraq we oversaw the torture of prisoners who were whipped, beaten, raped, hung from hooks, electrically drilled, humiliated in the nude, and urinated upon. None of that matters, so we imprisoned and tortured the Wikileaks 'torture whistle-blower', Private Manning too.

*

58

President Andrew Jackson

President Andrew Jackson was an asshole who killed and lied his way to power. From Tennessee lawyer, to soldier, and military officer he helped kill many Indians during the Creek War of 1813–1814. The Treaty of Fort Jackson required the Creek Indians surrender their lands (Alabama and Georgia). Jackson also helped win the Battle of New Orleans, against Britain, making him a national hero. Then Jackson led troops in the First Seminole War, which helped produce the Adams–Onís Treaty of 1819, and helped get Florida from Spain. Jackson briefly served as Florida's first territorial governor before winning election to Congress as a Tennessee Senator.

As president from 1829 to 1837, Andrew Jackson claimed to "advance the rights of the 'common man' against a corrupt aristocracy" and to preserve the Union. He helped found the Democratic Party based on those liberal platitudes, but during his lifetime Jackson owned a few hundred slaves. Jackson's behavior in the 'Dickens duel' outraged many who called it a "brutal, cold-blooded killing". Jackson ('Old Hickery') had a reputation as a violent, fiery, and vengeful psychopath.

Jackson met with many Indian tribes and would make fake treaties, that white immigrants had no intention of keeping; to encourage Natives to give up their lives as hunter-gatherers and take up farming, which fit better with the European immigrant way of life. Southern tribes included the Choctaw, Creek, Chickasaw, Seminole, and Cherokee. Northwest tribes included the Chippewa, Ottawa, and Potawatomi. Congress passed the Indian Removal Act, which Jackson signed into law. Jackson's presidency marked a new era in American Indian genocide by European immigrants, creating a 'Trail of Tears' for those tribes Between 1830 and 1850. American economic history hinged on the 'Trail of Tears'. Mass agricultural slavery of the South and predatory industrial Capitalism of the North depended on removal of Natives and their culture.

Jackson may have removed some corrupt officials, but his best failed effort was to call for the abolition of the Electoral College by constitutional amendment in his annual messages to Congress. Jackson also believed that the Federal Bank was a corrupt monopoly whose stock was mostly held by wealthy foreigners, and only benefited the rich. In 1833 Jackson began removing federal deposits, so money-lending functions were taken over by many local and state banks that 'popped-up' across America, thus drastically increasing credit and speculation. The 19th-Century cyclical economy of 'boom and bust' was following its regular pattern, but Jackson's financial measures contributed to the Crash of 1837. His destruction of the 'Second Bank of the United States' had removed restrictions upon inflationary practices of state banks; so wild speculation based on easy bank credit swept the newly conquered lands.

To reduce increased speculation (inflation), Jackson issued the 'Specie Circular' executive order that required buyers of Native lands (US 'owned') to pay in 'specie' (gold or silver coins). The result was high demand for specie, which many banks could not meet in exchange for notes, causing the 'Panic of 1837' and a deep depression. It took years for the economy to recover, and the bulk of the damage was blamed on Van Buren. Hundreds of banks and businesses failed during the Depression that followed. Thousands lost their lands in the next five years. The US was hit by the worst economic depression since it was founded in 1776.
President Jackson did some good things, with banks and parties; but he was a slave holder and Indian killer who signed laws to remove Native Americans permanently. Jackson waged savage war on tribes that were defending their own lives and lands.

President Trump compares himself to President Andrew Jackson; which one was more of an asshole? You decide. Jacksonian Democrats were similar to Trump Republicans in some ways; please investigate for yourself, to compare and contrast, and mail your essays to SCOD if you want us to publish your opinions for you.

*

Charles Dickens

Charles J.H. Dickens (1812-1870) was a famous English author who greatly influenced American society by exposing massive wealth inequality during the 1800s.

Dickens left school to work in a factory when his father was jailed in a debtors' prison. Dickens began professional editing, despite not having a formal 'higher education'. Dickens' literary success began with the 1836 serial publication of 'The Pickwick Papers'. He edited a weekly journal for 20 years, wrote 15 novels, hundreds of short stories and many non-fiction articles. Dickens lectured, wrote letters, and championed children's rights, education, and progressive reforms.

Barely literate poor people chipped in half-pennies for each monthly episode read to them, allowing the lower-class affordable material besides newspapers to read. His 1843 novella, 'A Christmas Carol', remains popular and continues to inspire royalty-free adaptations. <u>David Copperfield</u>, <u>Oliver Twist</u>, and <u>Great Expectations</u> are also still in popular consciousness. His 1859 novel, <u>A Tale of Two Cities</u>, set in London and Paris, is considered a classic historical fiction.

The term 'Dickensian economics' is used to describe policies reminiscent of his writings, because they benefit villainous predatory capitalist characters in stark industrial settings with poor victims of abuse (orphans and widows).

In America he addressed international copyright laws and the pirating of his work. The press popularity he gained caused a shift, and he became a cultural commodity. Dickens assumed the role of a responsible social commentator, publicly and in his writing; as a service to humanity.

He was a witness to the poor conditions of people in factories, institutions, and schools. Dickens resolved to "strike a sledge hammer blow" for the poor. Charles Dickens admitted to being very emotional regarding the issues in his writing, and would wander many nights in meditation, "when all sober folks had gone to bed". Dickens even founded a school for the 'redemption of fallen' lower-class women, named 'Urania Cottage'.

Dickens' novels were initially serials in weekly and monthly magazines, then reprinted in standard book formats: The Posthumous Papers of the Pickwick Club; The Adventures of Oliver Twist; The Life and Adventures of Nicholas Nickleby; The Old Curiosity Shop; Barnaby Rudge: A Tale of the Riots of Eighty; A Christmas Carol; The Life and Adventures of Martin Chuzzlewit; Dombey and Son; David Copperfield; Bleak House; Hard Times: For These Times; Little Dorrit; A Tale of Two Cities; Great Expectations; Our Mutual Friend;...

*

In politics there are 2 agendas: Utopia or Dystopia.

"That is just the way it is."
- *most people regarding slavery in the 1850s*

Systems of Abuse

When a liar has used their power to destroy your way of life and actively seeks to harm you further, you can feel love for them, but do not allow them to use love against you to keep you enslaved to abuse. This is the lesson of Battered Wives. I am not going to name names, but I know women that tell me their stories of staying in abusive relationships for too long. Civilization has allowed abuse in all systems for too long. I want to hear the voices of the brave, that speak out against injustice!

Peace, Love, and Freedom ARE the reasons to overthrow tyrants. Peace, love, and freedom are not just reasons to stay home and bake cakes, although that is nice too. Baking a Love cake for the masses doesn't do any good, if abusive plutocrats eat it all. Baking the cake and lovingly sharing it does not stop a bully or an enemy from hurting you. Sugar and honey help, but if you lovingly can defend yourself and use some anger to keep them from stealing or hitting, and find ways to sustain that peace, while still wishing them well; more peace, love, and freedom can flourish. Abusive people should not be in positions of power, and certainly not given militaries, secret agencies, and the ability to take everything away from others.

"If it is correct that a fundamental element of human nature is the need for freely creative work, without the arbitrary limiting effect of coercive institutions, then it will follow that a decent society should maximize the possibilities for this basic characteristic to be realized." - *Noam Chomsky*

During historic times of economic stress, people either turn on each-other or help each-other. Our system runs on Philosophy, aka theories of practice. Laws or only enforced through theories of belief by those who believe it is their job to act on or ignore lawyers are based on the ancient Greek philosophers called Sophists men who taught how to convince others they know what is TRUE.

Corporations are Capitalist groups of people seeking to benefit from taking from others, and giving less in return. Legal extortion is 'taking more than is fair', aka profiting by predatory trade; so this is why Capitalism does not work well with democracy. Our economic system needs to prey on workers so that companies can grow big enough to beat all others by keeping profits, and taking from most to give to the few in charge.

CEO's having totalitarian control of their workers and product sales, is not what is good for the people at large. These 'problems of power' are not taught very well, because so many people are not able to identify propaganda in mass media.

Yes a business can be ethical, but unless they are unethical enough to keep most wealth rather than sharing, they will never have any significant power in a system that rewards a person or group better for hoarding money. Making money means nothing, if you give it away as soon as you make it, in our system; we give most rewards to those that give or share the least.

Commercials we see on TV, are very similar to main-stream two-party politics; there is an illusion of choice but a command to buy. The shows serve the commercials, as entertainment between the more important segments of sponsor content. Both TV and Politics are backed by Corporations, but one of them is more honest about it. Guess which is more honest, TV or Politics? Yes, the annoying commercials on TV are more honest than our government about who funds a channel (party), and also who controls content; the more money, the more control. Companies like Exxon can not only control NPR and PBS, but also as we can clearly see under Trump, company bosses are consultants and government agents which claim to be beholden to 'the people', but clearly are owned by big business.

*

Talk It Out, SCOD Life Counseling & Coaching Service:
Existential philosophy & psychology with Dr. Drogo
Empedocles, SCOD Architect. Got a problem? Message a
request for talk counseling, donate to SCOD non-profit, then call
us and we will help you with whatever life issues you want to
talk about. We can help you balance your life in general, or
focus on troublesome details. Mentoring subjects: life, careers,
relationships, love, anger, finances, art, writing, religion, history,
architecture, gardening, and many more! SCOD Counselors:
Drogo Empedocles MA, Aeyla of the Hill People, TBA.
Schedule some hours with us to "talk it out". All counseling is
confidential.

Do you have vital life questions?
Do you want help weighing decisions?
Do you need career advice?
Message us and talk it out!

By donating to SCOD, you will have access to professionals in
many fields, under the direction of adviser Dr. Drogo
Empedocles. Doctor Reverend Drogo Empedocles has a
Spiritual Doctorate in Life & Death (Licentia Ubiquie Docendi
2015), a Masters Degree in Architecture (SCAD 2000), and a
license with the Universal Life Church; with minor studies in
environmentalism, historic preservation, philosophy theories,
relationship psychology, social dynamics, conservative finances,
alternative education, visual arts, creative writing, musical
composition, video editing, and organic gardening. Drogo was
the author of several books including Way Too Much, Harpers
Faery Magic Bible, SCOD Thesis, and many more titles.

Aeyla of the Hill People is a care-giver professional worker in
the State of Maryland; with minor studies in environmentalism,
relationship psychology, social dynamics, conservative finances,
special needs, and visual arts.

The rise of wealth inequality is a boiled frog phenomenon. Like a large slow rising bubble over everyone. Perhaps we need to find an economic way to value the lives of citizens. We have no other way to value human life with a quantifiable method.

International systems can demand some wealth equality as a basic right by law. True equality and freedom are only verbal platitudes if not defended legally. 'All humans are created equal' is deeper than just a verbal expression. The meaning of 'all men are created equal' is worth considering for anyone interested in what it means to be an enlightened American that understands what our founding fathers were talking about.

Chrystia Freeland

There has always been some gap between rich and poor in this country, but in the last few decades, what it means to be rich has changed dramatically. Alarmingly, the greatest income gap is not between the 1% and the 99%; but within the wealthiest 1 percent of our nation, as the merely 'wealthy' are left behind by the rapidly expanding fortunes of the new global super-rich. Chrystia Freeland, an acclaimed business journalist who has spent nearly two decades reporting on the trans-global elite, cracks open the tight-knit world of the plutocrats and proves that it is the wealthiest 0.1 percent who are outpacing the rest of us at breakneck speed. Best of all she begins to explain how their wealth affects everyone in good and bad ways.

In 2005 **Robert Reich** said that Bill Gates and Warren Buffet have the same amount of wealth as the bottom 40% of the US population, 120 million people. Does that mean that all men are created equal, but some really deserve a lot more if they figure out ways to legally take it from others? If it is true that we believe that money should only go to those that deserve it, we might want to make that clearer in our Declaration.

Do we think that many of the rich have really 'earned' it all, meaning they have earned enough to make millions of people jobless and homeless if they want? Should the rich have the right to keep all that money from those that could use it to create their own businesses; just as banks tend to do? What exactly qualifies the rich deserving to 'earn' power over millions of people? I do not see how anyone's personal story can justify the value divide of millions of lives. Oxfam and I agree on this; while that is nice some give back, there is a fundamentally larger problem of wealth inequality. On a positive note about Gates and Buffet, it is always good to know that some people have a bit of a social conscience, and when they give some of their god-like power back, yes it is nice.

'How Our Changing Environment Requires A New Definition Of Citizenship'

"Imagining what citizenship might mean in such an era is tricky, not least as it means thinking across both borders and generations. But there are mechanisms for attempting to balance the rights and responsibilities of individuals, nation states and our cosmopolitan obligations to a shared biosphere." - *Newsweek*

Imagine a love and peace based economy and government, yes it starts within. Economies and laws are ideas put into theories, which then work as mass philosophy & psychology based systems. We the people are ultimately responsible for our own leaders. SCOD plans towards anarchist collectives based on Love and Peace. We are open to hearing various dreams or seeing alternative visions. It is interesting to hear prophetic stories. Regardless of what you believe, or what comes true, everyone has a story to tell.

A primary question for Modern Economics should be
"Do we think that plutocrats should share our own nation's wealth with us more?"

Brexit was a symptom of the same systemic problem with Capitalism we are having in America. We are learning that England and Scotland are experiencing the same economic-political problem as us. The Scottish economist Mark Blyth says in both our countries it is the same capitalist problem; that the plutocrats will keep lowering wages by buying political parties. Unless the people UNIONIZE and threaten strikes everywhere, the rich will keep their money, and not give us our living share.

Professor Blyth says the Euro is a sinking luxury liner ship, and the investors want first class seats. If Scotland were to try to bring up their economy using the Euro again, Germany would do to them what they did to Greece. So things may not get better, unless we get more serious fast; same with the environment. Green and Civil Rights movements connect on resources available. All the people that have been saying they don't care about politics, or "just accept the way things are", need to help form protest unions. I think more people are waking up. If more women had political power we would have less wars; not just because women tend to be more loving, but because more active average people are loving than greedy corrupt elites, plus women make babies so they might care more about their future.

Yes power corrupts, the more it is monopolized, but if you spread the power democratically, share the wealth of a nation with its own people more, and distribute luxuries to bring the lowest and highest towards the middle, instead of the rich pushing the low lower, so only the few rich can get higher.

"Women are more emotionally unstable" is silly stereotype joke, but they do also tend to be more caring and loving. I was going to make the joke that women should have a few days off every month. But seriously, we need to distribute power and wealth to the people more fairly. No one should have the power Trump is trying to wield, even for good causes. It is the 'ONE RING' deal!

What is the Nation's Wealth, and who does it belong to? This a good question for a book focusing on economics. Notes based on talks: less jobs, more robots, how will people live with no income? Do private land owners have the right to ruin the lands of a country at the expense of a majority?

Many of us say that our National Wealth belongs to the people; much like our public lands. It seems more time should be spent socially discussing the meaning of public property. Perhaps we could make new words to fit enlightened concepts, like 'owner-sharing'. Cooperative efforts require negotiation, and common ground. We can look to the past for some guidance.

I was friends with a Greek economist, who conveyed to me in several messages and songs, how his country was suffering. I believe many Greeks believe in democracy and worker unity, but their neo-con leaders are bailing out their plutocrats with loans, while the poor get nothing. Sound familiar?

Dr. Alkistis Agio another Greek friend of mine, who speaks on behalf of Athena and Aphrodite to inspire many people to gain knowledge and happiness by following their dreams, finding their bliss, meditations, and practicing wisdom, peace, and love.

America may be the most powerful country in the World because of our military, but we are not the richest. In 2017 we are 5th richest according to Gross Domestic Product (GDP per capita at nominal values). America is 13th (GDP per capita PPP) according to International Monetary Fund data.

*

Enlightenment Philosophers

The philosophers of the Enlightenment were inspirations for the Founding Fathers of America. Some great Enlightenment thinkers include Diderot, Descartes, Hobbes, Spinoza, Locke, Leibniz, Hume, Rousseau, Kant, and Voltaire. They were freelance philosophers often working independent from the universities, challenging main-stream views. They had radical views on religion, politics and morality. They were dangerous rebels, one word away from exile, prison, or execution.

Descartes worked on mechanical and mathematic rationalism. He brilliantly said "I think therefore I am." However he based existence on a belief in God, who's 'maker's mark' is the idea of infinite as a concept that only God could make. Many founding fathers of America were also often Deists, but a century later wanted religion and churches out of politics.

Thomas Hobbes was an absolute monarchist, but his 'liberal' theories supplied ground work for American concepts of individual rights and limited government, as later expressed by Locke and Jefferson. Hobbes is paradoxically the father of Classical Liberalism. Thomas Hobbes explored the interrelations of government and economics, using linguistic inventions like 'Homo economicus'. 'Homo economicus' meant that ideal 'human nature' had an infinite ability to make rational decisions.

Hobbes assumes this hopeful idealistic attitude about people, despite basically being the Machiavelli of the 1600s. The Leviathan was his major political-economic concept, based on his experience during the English Civil War (1642-1651). His platonic strong-man authoritarian ideal, insisted that we need authoritative states to facilitate our higher potential nature; without which we will devolve into a "war of all against all" chaos in anarchy.

Hobbes argued that when we do not have a powerful entity impossible to disobey, human lives will only be "solitary, poor, nasty, brutish, and short."

If political theory had stopped evolving with Hobbes, 'Liberal' may have meant only Centrist Right-wing. Fortunately a man named John Locke had some additional thoughts on the subject. Locke's main point about human nature distinguished his own theories from Hobbes, which was necessary being from a younger generation who wanted to take another step in the name of 'progress'. Locke's definition of 'human nature' is a state of freedom tending towards social equilibrium. John Locke described a natural human instinct for rights of property, which would always naturally also result in seeking justice.

Locke argued that government must be founded on the consent of the people, and political power should be organized constitutionally into something like a system of separation of powers and checks and balances. Locke worked on social-contract constitutional theory.

David Hume died in 1776, the year of American Independence. Hume was a Scottish philosopher, historian, economist, and author; who wrote about the philosophies of empiricism, skepticism, and naturalism. David Hume had a very epicurean psychology; as he believed we are more influenced by our feelings, than reason. If we can embrace that fact, we can be stoically calmer and reasonably happy. Trying to be over-rational is a type of madness. We are a continuum of perception bundles. Utility of behavior is not the same as perfectly rational; because being good or 'reasonable' means experiencing patterns of feeling happy, and practicing habits that bring happiness. Hume believed in being social and happy in society.

In political-economics, Hume had a quantity theory of money, and a quality theory of politics; the later which should embrace intellectual wit, social sympathy, and respect or at least manners.

Hume's essay 'Balance of Trade' was an early economic theory model. Hume believed in some distribution of property, but perfect equality would deny pursuits in thrift, industry, or luxury. Perfect equality is impossible, but perhaps we can have a fairer slightly more equal system. Adam Smith was inspired by Hume. Hume had an ethical common-sense to his skeptical writings that Thomas Paine may have been inspired by, when he wrote our 'Common-Sense' revolutionary pamphlet.

Thomas Paine was an English-American political activist, philosophy theorist, and revolutionary. Paine was one of our Founding Fathers of the USA, and authored the two most influential propaganda pamphlets at the start of the American Revolutionary War. His ideas reflected Enlightenment era Classical Liberal writing on natural human rights.

Paine was a journalist by profession, and a propagandist by inclination. Paine was aided by Benjamin Franklin to migrate from Norfolk England, to the British American colonies in 1774. Many American rebels read or heard a reading of his seditious pamphlet 'Common Sense' (1776). Paine's 'American Crisis' (1776–83) was a pamphlet series for independence. John Adams said, "Without the pen of the author of Common Sense, the sword of Washington would have been raised in vain."

Paine lived in France for most of the 1790s, deeply involved in the French Revolution. He wrote 'Rights of Man', and soon made French political enemies, in addition to conservative British enemies. While in French prison, he continued to work on The Age of Reason (1793–94). James Monroe used his diplomatic connections to get Paine released in 1794.

Thomas Paine also published 'Agrarian Justice' (1797), discussing the origins of property, and introduced the concept of a guaranteed minimum income. Paine returned to America, where he died infamous for his ridicule of religion in 1809.

Voltaire primarily saw himself as a dramatic writer, he did not call himself an economist, but he did understand that France was flooded by debt financing. The French monarchy covered its exposure by manipulating inflation, insider bank deals, lowering wages, and raising taxes on the poor while the cost of living went up. Voltaire's base of operations was on the Swiss border, where as a business entrepreneur he diversified in agriculture, tanning, ceramics, real-estate, textile milling, and a watch-making enterprise with hundreds of employees. He combined laisser-faire with state capitalism (dirigiste protectionism).

Voltaire was a fan of Adam Smith, and wrote about many areas of new economic science. At the same time that he was fighting against civil injustice, Voltaire the business man was fascinated by the workings of high finance, and systems to rectify the mistakes and miscalculations of governments.

Voltaire believed that when a government only borrows from its own people, "confidence and the circulation of wealth are sufficient to ensure repayment". By lending to itself, the state promises to reimburse its own people, creating a perpetual debt of servitude, which can be renewed periodically. Voltaire died in 1778, 2 years after the USA was founded. For all his genius, ironically for many years Voltaire was no fan of democracy, which "propagated the idiocy of the masses"; and was in favor of the platonic concept of a philosopher monarch, until his noble benefactors disappointed him; after-wards suggesting perhaps "It is up to us to cultivate our garden", after-all.

Regarding Rousseau's radical writings in France, Voltaire was very critical. Voltaire called the "knave's" work immature, silly, and sorrowful. Regardless of Voltaire's dislike of Rousseau, the former King of France had considered them both to be his undoing. Rousseau beheaded King Louis, but continued state political violence, which ended up contradicting the declaration and constitution he had helped to create.

Adam Smith was a Scottish economist, philosopher, and author. He was a pioneer of political-economics, and was a key figure during the Enlightenment Era. Smith is best known for two classic works: <u>Moral Sentiments</u> (1759), and <u>Wealth of Nations</u> (1776). The Wealth of Nations, was the first modern work of Economics. Smith studied and taught social philosophy at the University of Glasgow. Smith collaborated with David Hume, and laid the foundations of neo-classical free-market economic theory. Academic belief in Mercantilism (state trade) began to decline in in the late 18th-Century. During the Industrial Revolution, Smith's writings helped merchants and monarchs embrace free-trade laissez-faire economics. The British Empire used its power to spread the new business model around the world, with more open markets and international trade.

Smith developed the concept of division of labor, and expounded upon how rational self-interest and competition can lead to economic prosperity. Smith was controversial in his own day. Adam Smith, the father of Capitalism, thought that there should be a way to take care of the poor, that capital & labor were intertwined. Smith and Paine were free-market supporters, but if they saw the predatory capitalism that exists today, they probably would consider it more powerful than the monarchies they fought against.

John Adams thought Paine was a dangerous person, because democracy was used in a pejorative sense until Paine began using it. John Adams was an American rebel who served as the second President of the USA (1797–1801). Adams was a lawyer, diplomat, statesman, politician, and, as a Founding Father, a leader of the movement for American Revolution.

John collaborated with his cousin, Samuel Adams. After the Boston Massacre, John Adams provided an unpopular legal defense of the accused British soldiers, in the face of severe local anti-British sentiment and driven by his devotion to the right to defense counsel. Adams was a Massachusetts delegate to the Continental Congress. John Adams wrote <u>Thoughts on Government</u>, and assisted Thomas Jefferson in drafting the Declaration of Independence in 1776. As a diplomat in Europe, he acquired vital government loans from Amsterdam bankers.

As president, John Adams encountered fierce criticism from Jeffersonian Republicans, as well as the dominant faction in his own Federalist Party, led by his rival Alexander Hamilton. Being strong on military defense, Adams built up the American Navy. John Adams was the father of John Quincy Adams, the sixth President of the United States. He died on the 50th anniversary of the Declaration of Independence, and the same day as Jefferson.

James Madison was an American statesman Founding Father, who served as the fourth President of the USA (1809 to 1817). James Madison served the Virginia House of Delegates. This "Father of the Constitution & Bill of Rights", like other hypocritical rebel leaders, owned hundreds of slaves.

James Madison collaborated with Alexander Hamilton and John Jay; producing 'The Federalist Papers', a Constitutional treatise. Madison's political views changed; he broke with Hamilton and the Federalist Party in 1791, then he and Thomas Jefferson organized the Democratic-Republican Party. Madison sought balance between federal and state governments. As with both Washington and Jefferson, James Madison left the presidency poorer man than when elected. His plantation financially declined, due to deflation and bad luck in business.

Alexander Hamilton died in 1804, but his political-economic theories supported banking and industry, which a century later became national economic policy, after 1861. Hamilton firmly supported government intervention in favor of business. Hamilton opposed free-trade, in favor of state capitalism (economic protectionism). As the first Secretary of the Treasury, Hamilton funded states' debts by the Federal government bank.

Being fiery, he supported a strong bully executive, for the US administrative republic. Alexander Hamilton believed that without dominant leadership to force federal policy, republican government would dissolve into state democracy.

*

French Revolution

In 1780 French commoners were angry with their ruler, King Louis XVI; and the way nobles ran their country. Although the government economy was suffering, nobles still lived in luxury and paid no taxes. Meanwhile the peasants and workers had to pay high taxes, relative to what they made, and there was not enough work or income for them all because the upper classes were keeping all the money. By 1789 the economy was broken, and the nobles called a meeting with the middle class.

The middle class demanded that nobles pay taxes at least, but the nobles refused. This made the French masses of commoners furious. A crowd of poor people helped by soldiers, attacked and captured a large prison called the Bastille. After the storming of the Bastille, many other lower classes rebelled in other areas, the middle class took control, and most of the nobles were executed in a period known as the 'Reign of Terror'. The military rage needed for the revolution, led to years of war campaigns and promoted war mongers like Napoleon, as greed and power was transferred and allowed to remain unchecked by humanitarian ethical philosophies. This is why revolution is never enough, if the natural tendencies of abuse and neglect are not addressed.

Vive la Revolution!

*

Marxism

Karl Marx saw Capitalism as an historic stage, which would stagnate due to internal contradictions, and would eventually be followed by Socialism and Communism. Karl Marx did not advocate a strong authoritarian state.

Communism usually means a state communist political system that uses either a state capitalist economy, or a libertarian socialist economy. Russia and China used a state capitalist economy, rather than allowing workers to control the economy, as true Marxist Communism advocates. Politically communism literally means a society that uses communal 'shared spaces', publicly owned (see Plato and Jesus), regardless of economics.

Socialism usually means a state capitalist social service system. Socialism is a political-economic theory of social organization that advocates production, distribution, and exchange should be owned and regulated by the population as a community. Marx suggested socialism could be a transitional state between the decline of capitalism, and the realization of communism.

Social political revolution will want an egalitarian classless society, when people feel what real liberty means.

Marxists define capital as an unfair economic relation between people, which is an out-dated tool to benefit the few with capital. Marx believed that private ownership of the means of production enriches capitalists at the expense of workers; so factories should be publicly owned by worker collectives.

Many of the problems of monarchy were not solved with Capitalism, because 'the rich get richer, and the poor get poorer' to the same degree ultimately, under either state controlled system. CEO company owners do not share work responsibility, and therefore dissociatively exploit the workers.

According to Karl Marx, capitalists would accumulate more and more capital, impoverishing the working class, thus creating social political-economic conditions for revolutions that would overthrow the institutions of capitalism. Private ownership over the means of production and distribution means masses of non-owner dependency on a ruling owner class, in opposition to human freedom which is a natural right.

A strong state is a cage, which should keep citizens safe from predators. Ideally we want an expanded fence so we can enjoy liberty, while also keeping us safe. Unfortunately bullies will make up threats and lie about enemies to keep power. So individual responsibility and awareness of problems is important, and should be studied more.

*

Post-Modern Capitalism

The 1% get their corporate hand-outs publicly with crony deals, to show you who to obey, granting you hopes that you will get lucky too. The only problem with those luck odds, are that the chances are not in your favor. Liberating thought from dogmatic straitjackets does not come with job security.

CEO to worker ratio wage discrepancy: 475-to-1

Capitalism works fine, just like Communism, in very small temporary controlled doses or temporary bubbles. Any system run perpetually will be 'gamed' or rigged by the players, and the one's with the most money when the music stops wins. At this point it is clear that the rich plutocrats are hoarding most of every nation's wealth, therefore the end result after centuries of capitalism seems to be the same as with monarchies, a very few people benefit greatly while the rest, the masses, live increasingly in disproportionate poverty.

These conclusions are based on the 'Lucas Critique' Theory and public statistics that are accepted by a majority of professionals in politics, business, and economics. Another symptom of the failure of capitalism is the rise of populism on the Right and Left, World-wide.

Thomas Piketty is the modern French economist that provided public charts to show income and wealth inequality in Europe and the USA. According to a New Yorker article, Piketty warns that "the New World may be on the verge of becoming the Old Europe of the twenty-first century's globalized economy." Piketty explains that while some inequality is inherently a driving force for capitalism, too much inequality is destructive for democracy, and will stop growth in capitalism as well, and can lead to decline in civilization. Economist Paul Krugman explained Piketty's data in writings and interviews, and discusses how the United States is becoming an oligarchy; the very system our founders revolted against. Comedian Steven Fry said "It is funny that countries that were monarchies, are more egalitarian today than America." Indeed it is ironic, that according to Piketty's charts, in the past 100 years we have switched power roles with Europe. (Piketty chart at end of book)

"Criticism of Capitalism - ranges from expressing disagreement with the principles of capitalism in its entirety, to expressing disagreement with particular outcomes of capitalism. Among those wishing to replace capitalism with a different method of production and social organization, a distinction can be made between those believing that capitalism can only be overcome through revolution (e.g. revolutionary socialism) and those believing that structural change can come slowly through political reforms (e.g. democratic socialism). Some critics believe there are merits in capitalism, and wish to balance it with some form of social control, typically through government regulation (e.g. the social market movement)." - *Wikipedia*

Capitalism & Sustainability

One of the main modern criticisms of capitalism is related to production-consumption commodity chains. These commodity chains refer to the network of material and commodity transfers of the global capitalist system. Such processes, all of which produce pollution and waste resources, are an integral part of the functioning of capitalism. Sustainability critics note that the statistical methods used in calculating 'Environmental Footprint' for industrial companies, may not consider all the factors, like ecological scale or perpetual population growth.

Our commercial market promotes environmentally irresponsible consumption and production. Under the "grow or die" modern mantra, there is little reason to expect hazardous consumption and toxic production practices to change significantly any time soon. Politics is always slow to popular movements, based on the power structure of the system.

Emma Goldman denounced wage slavery by saying: "The only difference is that you are hired slaves instead of block slaves." Authors of 'An Anarchist FAQ' state that anarchists have long recognized capitalism is hierarchical. The worker is subjected to boss authority. They state that "This hierarchical control of wage labor has the effect of alienating workers from their own work."

Capitalism treats labor as analogous to commodities, denies the key distinction between labor services and resources or products. Labor cannot be separated from the laborer. Labor, unlike property, is endowed with the will (or spirit) of a human life. What is a human life worth economically?

Self-governing at home, in public, and at the work place is what Liberty means. Creative self-managed work is a natural human source of pride and joy. Wrestling for control or work with others is not always the best way to live life, because not everyone desires competition, as it can more often bring out the worst in people, despite sometimes driving some to do their best. Social stress harms mental health, and can lead to accidents at work, abuse at home, and public disruptions.

Accumulation of capital generates waste and abuse that require costly corrective regulatory measures. High-pressure advertising causes demand for products to be sold at a profit; thereby creating rather than satisfying economic demand.

Democracy is based on the idea that we can shape our system to better our own lives. In democracy even today, the burden of success is shared by groups of individuals. Greater success for all does not end with the lucky ones getting paychecks, it begins with voting to share what belongs to all of us, by natural rights.

*

Ethical Economics

Curiousity Stream TV has a special airing currently called 'Conscious Capitalism', regarding economic sustainability.

Even the Catholic Church forbids 'usury'. Catholic social teaching, according to 'Rerum Novarum' and 'Quadra-gesimo Anno', does not support political capitalism because it is considered too aggressively liberal and is against social justice. In 2013 Pope Francis criticized capitalism as a "tyranny" that judged human beings purely by their ability to consume goods. He said that the "dictatorship" of the global financial system and the "cult of money" were making people miserable.

Perhaps Christianity should go to the basic beginnings of what communities should mean. Main budget issues should be proportional to popularity using general democratic voting, and then let representatives design the program details, but keep their pay equal to the common secretary.

"The nation's wealth is in our children and our rivers and forests and grasslands, our nation's wealth is in our investment in the future, as material possessions are all fleeting, and the only thing that matters is making sure there is a world for future generations to live healthy and happily in." - *Beamer*

The unequal reason to Tax the Rich more, and tax the Poor less, is because the economic system is unbalanced and unfair in favor of the Rich. When you do not have enough money to pay your basic bills, the same portion is more detrimental than to someone who has more than enough to cover all their bills and taxes. The Rich take from others disproportionately.

SCOD Political & Economic positions:
Tax the Richest 10%, to bring them back to human levels of power, and cap the upper class. No income or property taxes on the poor. Cover everyone's basic right to live: shelter, food, water. Create new sustainable Green jobs that include the Arts. Cut and restructure the military budget & mission to create anarchist embassy jobs in the arts, and include more civilian humanitarian missions; lethal weapons are never to be used on citizens. Universal living wage, with inflation caps.

Finland and Sweden's economies have intense socialist programs in their democratic governments to help society. 'Living wage' is a concept that we need to explore more. If we can allow more people to have money, the cost of living must be kept down by standards, to avoid inflation which could hinder enjoyment of the national basic income. The legal means for those inflation restrictions, could be multifaceted.

Laws should be made for tax money to pay back, to every citizen, the same as is needed by the poorest person to live on. Seeing the bigger economic picture can help those of us suffering from lack of income. In the larger economy, most individuals have very little income or control over available wealth sources.

Perhaps an understanding of the system can at least help us to accept that many unfortunate aspects of life are currently beyond our ability to affect; but some ideas like democracy can benefit us more if we work towards that goal.

Rather than ask our-selves what keeps us going, we should ask what stops us from acting on our convictions or following our dreams. People don't take the time to think about what they are doing in life. They just consume what companies give us, using money from other companies.

We need people-power instead of commercial propaganda. I think this grass-roots democratic battle for power needs to happen in politics, but also in all disciplines and even in Hollywood. Millionaires become true leaders, as stewards of fan villages. SCOD micro-economies work if property can be sustained. So it all starts with friends being good friends, and sharing love and joy; responsible regardless of fame.

Strong Love overcomes Strong Hate by flow dissolving corruption, and considerate redesign based on the flow. The flow is people power (becoming populist majority) with Love and Peace as our home base. Small scale change first focused on love being contagious, can spread to mass scale. Engaging ourselves as individuals in local grassroots parties, in urban areas. That is how to restructure entire national systems. When hate instead of love develops, it destroys systems, without having a plan of what to do once the system is crashed (anarchy chaos brainstorms libertarian socialism).

I try not to generalize about groups, but for hate-based groups (Nazis, KKK, Alt-Right) I make an exception. Hate-based groups are made to war against others, Union-based groups are made to defend each-other against those that seek to divide and conquer our freedoms. There are reasons why Hitler is hated, and why good people cannot allow a leader like that to command or run systems of people.

Never forget: Fukushima, oil spills, Kent State, coal mine wars, Native American wars, American Revolution, Civil War, ...

We have had massive New York, CA, DC, Utah, and Rhode Island protests against corporate politicians. Conservative opponents of the protesters falsely claim the protesters were paid, and not legitimate. I would like to be paid to protest on my own behalf, too bad corporations are not going to fund the Revolution. Even if large protests could be funded temporarily, that will not determine how desperate people are for real political-economic change.

Real people are starting to hold their leaders accountable; internet social media is helping.

Sarcasm - "Dear scientists, detectives, investigators, and inspectors; popular opinion is that there are no real theories or conspiracies; so stop looking for proof. There is no proof that any conspiracy or theory ever really existed. Just kidding. Conspiracies are plans made by people, and theories are explanatory stories based on historic-fiction (evidence connected by assumptions). You never heard that no one ever conspired to do anything?" - *Dr. Mandelbrot Fizzles of Snark Enterprises*

*

Sexonomics

Matriarchy must grow and balance our existing Patriarchy. This revolution is rooted in Love and Peace, like arteries and veins permeating branches, and connected to our heart. Feminism and Hermes/Aphrodite rights are very critical today. I believe there are many types of relationships, friendship being most important. I tend to find that males can usually handle aggression better than females because of testosterone, but with gender such statements are of course generalizations.

I do think that civilization has operated on the chemical role differences found in military power systems, allowing men to dominate politics and religion as well. Predatory Capitalism also seems based on competitive aggression more than compassionate sympathy. These patriarchal power structures may be why cultures tend to be so homophobic; viewing feminine 'weaknesses' like love and care, as vulnerabilities that opponents can use against helpless victims.

I think many of our problems in the World today are a result of our inability to place humanitarian leaders in power, that would balance the lop-sided abusive 'titanic' systemic dynamic that has perpetuated demagogues over democracy.

*

Political Definitions

Although the term 'Right-wing' originated with traditional conservatives, monarchists, and reactionaries; the term 'extreme Right-wing' has also been applied to movements including fascists, Nazis, and racial supremacists. Right-wing politics justifies a hierarchical society on the basis of ideology or culture. Right-wing politics involves rejecting egalitarian objectives of Left-wing politics (equal civil rights). Right-wing ideologies support legal order under authoritarian states. The original French Right-wing was called "the party of order" and held that France needed a strong political leader to keep order.

*

WALL STREET

There are many films that address the modern predatory Capitalist greed that Wall Street exhibits: Wolf of Wall Street (2013), Equity (2016), Big Short (2015), Bonfire of the Vanities (1990), Dealers (1989), Trader (1987), Wall Street (1987), Trading Places (1983), It's A Wonderful Life (1946), ...

85

'Trading Places' Hypothesis of Wealth & Poverty;
Nature or Nurture?

'Nature versus nurture' summarizes a long-running debate on whether human behavior is determined by the environment during a person's life, or by their 'breeding' genes. Consensus seems to be that our lives are amalgams of nature 'AND' nurture. We are both a product of our environment and our biology.

Nature was the law of reality. Then the view that humans acquire behavioral traits from 'Nurture' was termed "tabula rasa" (blank slate) by John Locke in 1690. The phrase 'nature vs nurture' was popularized by the English Victorian polymath Francis Galton, discussing the influence of heredity and setting on social status. Galton 'father of genetics' was influenced by the book On the Origin of Species, written by his half-cousin, Charles Darwin. Mark Twain's 1881 'Prince & the Pauper' book's theme was 'nature vs nurture'. These two conflicting attitudes about human nature and development, were at the core of an ideological dispute over research agendas during the second half of the 20th century.

In a 2014 survey of scientists, many respondents wrote that the dichotomy of nature versus nurture had outlived its usefulness, and should be retired. In ecology and behavioral genetics, researchers think nurture has an essential influence on nature, and nature often defines our capacity for nurture. Rich pricks like Ben Carson often believe that poverty is at its core a state of mind; stating if you make a rich person temporarily poor, they have the mental capacity to become rich again, where as if you make a poor person rich, they will lose all their wealth. In the case of mentally or physically impaired people who cannot think in ways that make people money, yes their disability may be a detriment to their functionality. However, wise rich people know that the only real difference between them and poor people is LUCK; since the poor can have talent and work hard.

The plot example in the film 'Trading Places' shows that genetic 'nature' does not determine a person's place in society, but rather a person can stay in their class position by 'nurture' social conditioning and conditions. Our place in society is largely a result of a combination of circumstances we call life, in which good people can do bad things, and bad people can do good things. In 'Coming to America' the old formerly rich men from 'Trading Places' are still living homeless in the streets. When they get a government hand-out from the Prince of Zamunda (Eddie Murphy again), they say "we are back!".

Comedy, art, and weirdness and help relieve physical and intellectual suffering that society causes.

In a just society, we should be able to be open about our own finances, so that we can function in society appropriately in proportion to our means. When my income is low, I tell other people so they can help me get more income. Even if I am ashamed of having problems getting paid for my work, it helps to hear from another person having similar problems. It helps empathetic-ally and economic-ally. Honesty is of course important in a free-society; the problem of addicts who steal, and con-artists who prey on generous victims, will be understood to require psychological help.

Linguistic philosophy can help expose contemporary political problems, by defusing loaded terms (pun).
*

An Artist in Society

Artist: would you like to buy my art work?
Employee: No thanks, I can get art for free.
Boss: No, most art is gay.
Artist: Please will you reconsider? I have bills to pay.
Employee: I have bills to pay too, and things I WANT to purchase, and my boss doesn't pay me enough.
Artist: Instead of buying a commercial product, could you instead purchase my work?
Employee: You will have to wait until my next pay check, then maybe (this means NO).
Boss: I have more important things to do, but keep working and doing what I suggest, then one day, you can 'make it'.
In America you can be successful if you work hard enough, all the time, and keep at it.
Artist: I have been working hard all my life, I have even tried working tons of normal jobs just to pay the bills, but the chances of me being successful are very very slim, when you consider that the masses of artists do not earn any income, and as a cliche are kept poor by the perpetuating social stereotype. No one wants to pay for art, because the Capitalist market is saturated with art they monopolize and get profits from, at the expense of the consumer. I think if I continue to work hard, and keep struggling to achieve more, I will end up more miserable for having failed and hurt myself, because that is the fate of the masses, of which I am one.
Boss & Employee: Get a hair-cut, and a real job.
Artist: I have found out that I am an artist, not an employee, and I don't even want to boss other people around. Would you want me as an employee or a boss?
Boss & Employee: NO. Probably not.

*

88

Stocks and Bonds and Mutual Funds

When I contemplate which industrial giant I would be willing to put stock into, for mutual benefit to the best of my knowledge; the list is very short. Yes I could get economic gains with stock from corporations we all use every day, however when I ask if they help to pay my bills, the gain from stock over a few years is pitifully less than the bills I must pay every month, of which they support as part of the system. We put or keep the ones in power, in power, by giving them all our money.

Our government supports Wall Street more than the very lofty idea and surface voting system we call 'democracy'. In what appears to be the way in which we elect politicians, we go to a public place, at a certain time, and 'cast ballots'. What really happens is our Stock-Market Capitalist machine controls the politics. Funding campaigns is what puts the crony capitalists in place, and holds them accountable to their corporate interests. They use large donations to fund political campaigns, and then get more from lobbyists later privately, as well. The votes some make by purchasing stocks, have more power than actual political votes, when considering influence ratio differences. Gather greens, within your means. If you have no money, beans can supply your stocks, as they are cheap but powerfully high in protein.

Housing Bubbles

Location, location, location is such bullshit. Our family house was often considered prime real-estate, in a tourist location, on top of the hill, in a famous historic town, over-looking a national park, and yet it sold at a fraction of what the mansion sized home was worth. The banks refused to loan, because while they are earning record profits, they are not allowing middle-class people any gains. They say this is due to the risk of fore-closure if buyers cannot pay their mortgages, which makes no sense if in the next town closer to a big city property is even more expensive. Our cost of living is inflated.

Banks make poorer families pay huge appraisals and fees, indicating a bias in the market that decreases the wealth of lower middle-class and upper lower-class, making upward mobility much harder. People feel like killing other people over much smaller amounts of money than hundreds of thousands, so we should consider the actions of banks to be terrible for the system; not just 'unfair', but an injustice. Many of us are being cheated out of our life savings by those in power who could make a change to benefit home-owners but do not, for their own self-interests.

Business Parties

'Party' relates to business more than most people think, although we tend to portray party play as the opposite of work. Political parties are called parties for a reason; party groups are driven by popular emotions regarding social issues and personal freedoms. Millionaires use parties not only to relax, have fun, and to show off their wealth; but more importantly as part of their business strategies, regardless of atmospheric impressions or attitudes; the crazier the party, the more impressions affect social dealings afterwards, and bonds can be created, courted, or destroyed. The anticipation of enjoying parties is social and work reward enticement; and during a party the socializing is in a rare setting that allows for more intimate personal connections to be expressed and played out.

Parties, vacations, and breaks are important for rethinking things, healing with joy and relaxation, and reflecting on problems. Things can look very different when we return to them. Some solutions come during the in-between times.

*

Denis Diderot and His Encyclopedias

Denis Diderot (1713-1784) was a French philosopher, author, and artist. Diderot was a hero of the Enlightenment and is best known for serving as co-founder, chief editor, and contributor to the Encyclopédie. Denis Diderot earned a 'Master of Arts' degree in philosophy. Then he entered the University of Paris and studied Law. He abandoned the idea of joining Church clergy, and decided instead to become a writer. Diderot disliked being a lawyer, and was not into any professional business, so he was disowned by his father. For the rest of his life he was considered a bohemian.

Paris Salon thinking was radical, and expressing it was dangerous. Diderot was jailed for believing that knowledge comes from common senses and common people, not from the Church or aristocracy. Diderot was imprisoned for his writings, an experience that left him too scared to lay out his philosophy plainly; often disguising it within plays, novels and letters. Diderot's literary reputation during his lifetime rested primarily on his plays and encyclopedias. Voltaire called him the "Socrates of the Enlightenment". Diderot's expensive and rare books were banned, to which he said "A book banned, is a book read." Many of his important works were published after his death.

Diderot Quotes:
"The greatest good of the people is liberty.
Liberty is to the state what health is to the individual."
"Power gained by violence is only temporary usurpation."
"Reason is to the philosopher, as grace is to the Christian."
"Men will never be free until the last king is strangled,
with the entrails of the last priest."
"No one has the natural right to command other humans."
"Happiest are the people who give most happiness to others. "

*

Modern Minimalist Economics
"Less Is More." - *Mies van der Rohe*
"Your possessions do not define you or your success;
no matter what marketers will try to tell you". - *Becker*
"I live within my means." - *Warren Eng*

*

Wealth Warnings

"I am a product of birth, circumstance, and timing. I am rich and I am good at predicting. I see pitchforks." - *Nick Hanauer*

"I am not saying that wealth inequality is morally wrong, I am arguing that rising inequality is stupidly self-defeating and unsustainable, not just because of pitch-forks, but because it is bad for business too." - *Nick Hanauer*

Nick Hanauer is a rich guy, plutocrat, an unrepentant capitalist. He says he is one of the 0.01%. Nick has something to say to his fellow plutocrats: "Wake up!". Growing inequality is about to push our societies into conditions resembling pre-revolutionary France. Nick Hanauer argues that a dramatic increase in minimum wage could grow the middle class, deliver economic prosperity, and prevent a revolution. - *Ted Talks*

Our economy is like an eco-system, and should be made to maintain our actual ecosystem. For a fully functioning system we need full participation by the masses, not a predatory system eating itself. When consumers have no more money, they cannot buy products. When we use up all our natural and human resource capability with unsustainable growth consumption, we will have no environment to sustain human global ecology.

"The work of democracies is to maximize the inclusion of the many to create prosperity, not to enable the few to accumulate money." - *Nick Hanauer*

Nick Hanauer is proud to have earned money; so whether the rich have earned the majority of our National Wealth or taken it unfairly, the issue goes beyond pride. No matter how hard we work to get money, we are proud to have the money we get.

The total amount of money in the economy is more important than individual pride, and as a nation we can talk about who should have rights to hoard it. Yes some rich people give back some of their vast wealth, but they do not become mega-rich by equal earning or sharing fairly. Economists are saying that inequality is growing, and more people will become poor.

Wealth inequality is a macro-economic systemic issue. Rich vs Poor is not just confined to local jealousy, the Rich do wage war on the Poor by controlling politics and laws that keep wealth confined at the highest levels, rather than distributing power for all to share. The biggest reason why people may not see the problem, is that it has to do with how money is not as available to many people who do not communicate with each-other. Large sums of money are needed to start 'competitive' businesses, or they will be bought up or pushed out of the market by monopolies. Rich people have private reserve funds that common people are not able to access from stocks, banks, and other rich partner investors.

We are told if we cannot get money to survive it is our own individual problem alone, and government should not help common people (only the rich). The larger statistical picture proves that the poor only have limited control over their wealth. The probability that each one of us will have a chance to 'figure out how to make money' is decreasing according to professionals that study economics, including like Nick says, smart rich people that actually do care about sustainability.

So we are beginning to talk about strategies that make more sense to support human life, as a human right. Passing laws that support for the poor, tax the rich, and sustain greater wealth equality, will begin to give more weight to the words 'all people are created equal', since slavery was abolished officially by President Lincoln.

Rather than denying people the ability to 'earn a living' if they didn't get lucky enough to 'game the system' like the very few rich people, maybe we can allow poor people to at least live a basic life. The statistics of gambling is a fair metaphor for the overall economy, with odds increasingly against the middle-class and poor, as economic trends indicate according to the experts that study sustainable economics. It also has less to do with 'working harder' as many poor people have worked harder than many rich people. And there are many smart poor people, that are not able to earn money for various reasons. So I am trying to help people to begin to rethink some of the talking points we have been fed, because they do not hold true.

Semantic Hitmen

Earning and taking money are semantic synonyms; if one is paid to assassinate another, and it is carried out, one will both earn and take the money, and one can use one word for the other. How much is a human life worth? On social media we deal with many personal text fights about opinions of intelligence and integrity, but we try not to resort to name calling, because of matters of self-education for anyone with a conscience. It has taken me years of studying sustainability to collect data, which sadly is showing problems that some of us learned about in school are getting worse, for various reasons. My goal is to provide alternative solutions to the main-stream theory problems. Bernie Sanders and others have long understood that to make our country better, we need to know the problems. Sanders gives hope.

There are other theories out there for sure, but for ethical reasons, SCOD works with ones that would increase the standard of living for the majority, rather than only benefit a minuscule minority.

It comes down to simple finance math ultimately. The worship of the rich by the poor masses is not a new condition of civilization (debt or wage slavery), but technology and education are helping those with a social conscience to plan, create, and practice better egalitarian ways that can include more people in an economic ecosystem.

The tools to accomplish a 'new green deal' (or whatever we want to call the economic and political revolution) are the World-wide Web (using social media and information platforms), monetary digital transfer, time trading, service trading, goods trading, and the belief in non-monetary ethical value ideology involving Consciousness, Life, and fair work reciprocity.

Our peaceful revolution is dependent on education and practice of livelihoods across disciplines using those meta-tools. Anarchist and democratic human social nature has the ability to maintain egalitarian equilibrium, despite group bubble enclaves of hero worship that will occur from time-to-time. If the majority of people do not believe in the need for dictatorial 'strong-men', and people have direct political and economic power, then they will also have responsibility.

Our ability to practice these new methods of commerce are up to us, to accept the responsibility to create or move to local environments where we are able to believe and practice freely. Archeologists are finding that when empires decline, societies decentralize and network with less authoritarian control. When that kingly control occurs during a 'dark age', it is on a smaller scale, for a few hundred years.

Modern American Libertarians are not wrong about individual responsibility being vitally important in life. We should not be dependent on an authoritarian state government or super rich gods. It is and should be our responsibility to be able to provide for ourselves. Currently the super-rich and the government are taking away our abilities for the basics of living by means of a predatory system, so it is up to individuals to understand the issues, and see if there are some common problems. I am talking about water pollution and resource sharing, and many other factors which require new ways (old ways) of working together as a society.

National wealth and resources belong to the people, not the super wealthy who 'earned it all'. Another problem when talking to other average Americans, is our libertarian thinking that economics have nothing to do with politics in a State Capitalist system that clearly and legally facilitates crony capitalism.

In our system politics and economics are basically the same; and we must accept the reality of that, and take responsibility. To deal properly with that fact, and we want to increase standards for living and human rights for all people, then we must take action to give the democratic political power back to people through economics.

We want to increase the ability for people to be self-sufficient. There must be more ways for people to hunt and gather their own food. Gradual generational reduction of population would be a reasonable consideration in the future. Population growth is a factor few people want to consider, but perpetual growth of population and increasing resource consumption is factually unsustainable according to scientists that study urban planning. That means systemic stewardship of an economic ecology is necessary to sustain human life into the future.

It is ok if you believe or have your own theory, I just want to clarify what I am working on, regardless of who agrees. The terms are tedious, complicated, and often very confusing for most people. So I'm working on refining the ideas that my friends and associates have been talking about for years. Thank you for considering my words strung into sentences, and accumulated into paragraphs. What you consider the facts at various periods in your life, and what you believe based on your assumptions of facts, is all ultimately up to you.

We have been told by many that it is simply a dog-eat-dog world, and survival of the fittest means competitively always trying to one-up everyone else. We are like gaggles of children vying for parental attention. I am not writing to convince everyone of my beliefs. Many people are determined to wear business suits, or ties, and have life-long ties to big business; those people are bought and sold and their conditioned minds will not be changed freely by words for obviously selfish but beneficial reasons to them. I am writing for the rest of us, that believe that evolutionary survival can mean that the fittest will cooperate enough socially for more equal human rights for all.

Being 'the fittest' does not always require aggressive destruction and domination of others, but often in history has meant strength by nurturing inclusively compassionate relationships, in groups that care about each-other symbiotically. Those that disagree with valuing compassionate sharing over selfish greed, will always struggle to get their way so they can be the best, and feel that others deserve less because they are able to take more, but they depend on popular opinion for their power as well.

*

Comedy Vs Politics

The strong historical relationship between Comedy and Politics is evident, and still exists; despite word meaning fluctuation.

Comedy comes in many forms: live theatrical plays, recorded performances, visual cartoons, and several different types of comics and joke humor. Comedy meant something different to the Greeks, whose democracy developed from their communal and civic theater traditions that engaged active participation; based on an ancient oral bardic tradition, similar to the Celtic Druids. Politics classically means government by the people and for the people, but is now conventionally used to mean popular propaganda by state sponsored representatives.

Ancient Greeks began writing down comedy plays, riddled with social and political satire. I mention that they wrote them down, to note that historically before that, during their dark-age of political savagery, they had forgotten how to read or write for a few hundred years. Later after the fall of the Roman Empire, a similar dark-age occurred when most people again could not read or write. During the medieval Dark-Age at least beautiful gothic stained-glass and architecture provided some public function, and monasteries illustrated manuscripts. Some Modern popular economists believe that the feudal system was a period of economic growth, because the few wealthy elite nobles had plenty of wealth, and therefore benefited the masses by inspiring them somehow, despite their dirty peasant lives. However, sustainable economists will study the over-all wealth of the population and ecosystem, internal and external; holistically.

During the feudal 'middle-ages' a familiar character emerges in royal courts. We are all familiar with 'court jesters', or professional fools, as legendary establishment tricksters or clowns. Sometimes they may have been used by a ruler to mock opponents, but more interestingly the court jester mocks their own king in folk-tale stories. Regardless of historic basis, the concept of the fool that criticizes power persists in popular culture. Why is only a fool able to attack or publicly affect power? The reason that comedy affects power, is because political power is socially dependent, and under authoritarian leaders no one that participates in the system dependent on kissing the ring of power can publicly question or criticize those who they must court for influence.

Shakespeare helped to bring civilization into the period known as the Enlightenment. His plays were shaped by the dramatic literature that preceded him, as well as current events. Common audience members enjoyed performances they could understand, and so the satire was intended to be obvious to them. Despite some noble funding by loyal royal theater patrons, most audience members were lower class. There are social reasons the Merchant of Venice or Othello became famous; because beyond racism there were class economic forces driving competition and unrest. Today America has become a mirror image of the economic structure of European monarchy and the inequality that plagued the people, according to Piketty's economic analysis which is just now becoming popularly accepted as worth considering by society.

Jon Stewart and Stephen Colbert helped to shatter the illusion of crony corporate politics, and expose the political hypocrisy that their lies create, publicly. Stewart used the role of the 'simple fool', and Colbert used the role of the 'caricature artist'. They both used mockery and sarcasm to explain the news, and allow us to feel we are not alone in feeling powerless.

*

Peaceful Politics: Theory vs Policy
True Distinction of Left vs Right in Theory and Policy

SCOD Politics 101: The Left-wing goal is humanitarian freedom, the Right-wing objective is totalitarian military. Both can act like each-other to defend themselves, but those are the ideologies. The definitions apply to people based on the majority of their actions, not just words. Revolutionary Classical-Liberals are for individual rights like modern American Libertarians; a concept which should be considered Liberal and therefore Left-wing (corporations are not people), however selling out to corporate interests has made them more Right-wing.

Authoritarianism tends to be more Right-wing, and Egalitarianism tends to be more Left-wing. The Right still often accepts militant violence against protestors and enemies, while the Left has progressed towards non-violent means of resistance, control, and influence. Environmental Left-wing eco-terrorists tend to use less-than-lethal tactics, with some exceptions due to opposition infiltration or Right-wing influence in ideology. Many are confused by Neo-Liberal politics which is labeled 'Centrist'. Neo-Lib is actually Right-wing Neo-Conservative in supporting plutocracies over all civil liberties. Today corporate crony politics has made both wings Right-wing conservative for the plutocrats. In basic politics, the note to always end on is that politicians lie because they are actors playing the role of a social civil-servant for their corporations.

Peace by social progress is Left-Wing; Peace by military progress (War) is Right-Wing. Despite labels, anytime Leftists use violence, they become part of a Right-wing game. Those definitions are based on their theory ideologies in the pure form, but actual leaders or regime incarnations, being human, often hypocritically contradict their popular labels. This was the fate of 'State Communism' and the reason why global 2-party systems do not really have a true Left wing today. Terminology gets confused, as no side is purely one or the other. True Left means love, civil rights, compassion, non-violence; but because people think Communist states were Left due to ideology that was barely addressed under totalitarianism.... the words are confusing. Non-violence is vital to Leftist theory, and when Leftists are violent, they play into 'might is right'.

People who want to be on the Right today, seem to think Hitler was actually Socialist, aka Left, because of his party label. Hitler ran as a 'National Socialist'; this does not mean he actually was Left-wing, or did anything in accordance with Left ideology; it means Hitler was a demagogue liar that perpetuated militant totalitarianism and fascism under a false label.

There is incredible double-speak in politics, and I am seeing it in comment sections by citizens more and more. One cannot slaughter thousands of citizens around the World, rule by war, provide public works for only elite survivors, and be Leftist based on false platitudes. Those that use Right-wing violence cannot claim to be true Left-wing. This strange lack of educated understanding of theory makes no sense, when we explore all the terms for groups; and I believe has been used to lie to the public, to trick them into voting against their values. Neo-Nazis are clearly the opposite of hippies; they are two extremes of Right and Left in modern society. Hitler's actions were mostly extreme Right-wing militant and fascist, while true hippies are extreme Left-wing pacifists. Violent punks are Centrist to Right-wing in their actions when they fight or vandalize.

Major double-speak has been going on in the past few decades, and now under Trump. The confusion with the American Libertarian label has also perpetuated the bashing of the term 'Liberal' and now the Right is attempting to co-op it by claiming to be Patriotic like the founders, in their efforts to allow corporations and the 1% to rule us. To be fair, our American Revolutionary politics originally had much to do with slavery.

In political history the term 'Left' refers to the French Revolution anti-monarchist group members (Montagnard and Jacobin) of the 'Third Estate', who sat to the left of the main chair in parliament, a habit which began in the 'Estates General' of 1789.

Throughout the 1800's in France, the left was the Liberal Republic, and the right was the Conservative Monarchy. Nationalism, socialism, democracy, and anti-clericalism became features of the French Left. After Napoleon III's 1851 coup (Second Empire), Marxism began to rival republican utopian socialism within left-wing politics. The popular Communist Manifesto asserted that all human history is class struggle. That book's prediction that a worker's (proletarian) revolution would eventually overthrow bourgeois capitalism; terrified both capitalists and monarchists alike, as the communist revolution would remove them from power economically and politically. The corrupt leaders in Europe used the word 'Social' and Marxist theory in their platforms, only because they could never have gotten support from workers without it; therefore almost every party was using it. Strong men took over the dominant parties, and made totalitarian dictatorships that valued absolute law over control by the people. It was in this period that the word "wing" was appended to both Left and Right. Thus Left-wing theory helped create Right-wing regimes who used propaganda to lie to its own supporters, and valued State power above all else.

In the USA many leftist social liberals, progressives, and trade unionists were influenced by the works of Thomas Paine, who introduced the concept of asset-based egalitarianism, which theorized that social equality is possible by a redistribution of resources. It is incredible how Thomas Paine was left out after the Revolution by other Founding Fathers, to could implement a more authoritarian Federal government with kingly powers.

*

The Nazi political strategy grew out of the popular socialist politics of anti-big business, anti-bourgeois, and anti-capitalism; such aspects were later contradicted to gain the support of industrial owners. In the 1930s the party's focus shifted to anti-Semitic and anti-Marxist themes. The Nazi party deliberately drew workers away from communism and into nationalism. The term "Nazi" (National) derives from 'National-Sozialist', whose opposition party was Sozi (Social), 'Sozial-Democrat'.

Nazi party members usually referred to themselves as National-Sozialisten (National Socialists), rarely as "Nazis". The term Partei-genosse (party member) was commonly used among Nazis. In 1933, when Adolf Hitler assumed power of the German government, usage of the designation "Nazi" diminished in Germany; although Austrian anti-Nazis continued to use the term derogatorily.

The Nazi party grew out of smaller political groups with nationalist patriotic fervor formed in the years of World War I. Drexler had created a new political party and proposed it be named the 'Socialist Worker's Party', but Harrer objected to the term "socialist"; the issue was settled by removing the term and the party was named the German 'Workers' Party' (Deutsche Arbeiter-Partei, DAP). From the outset DAP was opposed to non-nationalist political parties on the Left. DAP leaders were bigoted against 'Bolshevism' and 'Jews'.

DAP was a small group, but attracted the attention of German authorities, who were suspicious of any radical subversive group. In July 1919 while stationed in Munich, Corporal Adolf Hitler was promoted to 'army intelligence agent' (Verbindungs-mann), by the head of the 'Education and Propaganda Department' in Bavaria, Captain Mayr. Hitler's assignment was to influence other soldiers and to infiltrate DAP.

Hitler always spoke about the same subjects: the Treaty of Versailles and 'the Jewish Question'. To increase its appeal to larger segments of the population and other groups (like the Socialists), in 1920 DAP changed its name to the 'National Socialist Workers Party'. The NSWP was referred to as the Nazi Party, by outsiders. A mutiny broke out within the Munich Nazi Party. Munich members of its executive committee, some of whom considered Hitler to be 'a tad' too aggressive, wanted to merge with the rival Socialist Party (DSP). Storm-troopers (SA) named 'Brown-shirts' were founded as a Nazi party militia in 1921, and began violent attacks on other parties.

Hitler's two main party goals were always German nationalist expansionism and anti-semitism. Nazi rallies were often held in beer-halls, where down-trodden men could get free beer. 'Hitler Youth' was formed for children of party members, a Nazi sub-sect which went main-stream in late 1920s.

In Italy a party with similar policies and goals came to power, called the 'National Fascist Party'; under a bigoted boss named Benito Mussolini. Fascist militia 'Blackshirts' (MVSN), terrorized any political resistance nation-wide. Mussolini later formed the OVRA, a secret police (like German SS) that had official state support. This is how the German and Italian dictators held their power. The Fascists, like Nazis, promoted national patriotic revival; which opposed Communism and Liberalism. These dominant Right-wing parties appealed to the working-class; suffering veterans who opposed the Treaty of Versailles; and advocated military and economic expansion of their government into other countries.

Hitler was inspired by Fascist style, imitating the use of their Roman straight-armed salute. Fascists came to power in 1922 with a coup attempt called the "March on Rome". Nazis used a patriotic beer-hall rally to launch their own attempted coup.

Munich army soldiers refused to support the extreme German Right-wing Nazi mob. Then Nazis staged a march of a few thousand through Munich to rally support. German army troops opened fire, and 16 Nazis were killed. Hitler and other party leaders were arrested, and tried for treason in 1924. The Nazis were given lenient prison sentences, during which time Hitler wrote his political manifesto / auto-biography called 'Mein Kampf' (My Struggle).

The Nazi Party was temporarily banned, but remained active with support from another German nationalist party. Hitler was released from prison, and the following year he reorganized the Nazi Party, with himself as the leader. The new Nazi Party and its militias were kept separate, and the legal aspect of the party's work was emphasized.

Nuremberg had a Nazi Party Rally in 1927. Rallies soon became massive displays of Nazi para-military power and attracted many recruits from the lower and middle-classes, who had suffered the most from inflation and shortages after WWI. German small business owners were receptive to Hitler's racism against Slavs and Jews, who they blamed for economic depression. The Nazi party had 130,000 members by 1929.

I could go on to talk about Nazi leaders like Hess, Himmler, Goebbels, and Göring; but tedious detail regarding Nazis gets terribly boring. The Nazi Party might never have come to power had it not been for the Great Depression and its effects on Germany. By 1930 the German economy was beset with mass unemployment and widespread business failures.

Social Democrats and Communists were bitterly divided, unable to unionize, so the Nazis took advantage using state terrorism. The Nazi '25 Point Program' was not Left-wing because the entire government was too Right-wing to implement it well.
Such ideas like "equality of rights" were ignored, and followers allowed totalitarian control. Some of it's tenets like "Common

national criminals, usurers, profiteers and so forth are to be punished with death, without consideration of confession or race." are clearly Right-wing. Right-wings represent abusers and the abused, accepting the traditional abuse pattern system on a moral basis; and Left-wings represent victims who want Justice for State ethical crimes. The notion of Totalitarianism as a 'total' state political power, was detailed by Amendola in 1923. He described Italian Fascism as a system poetically different from conventional dictatorships. Later the term 'Totalitarian' was assigned positive meaning by Gentile, Italy's leading theorist of Fascism. He used the term "totalitario" to refer to the structure and goals of the new state, which were to provide the "total representation of the nation and total guidance of national goals." Mussolini said "Everything within the state, nothing outside the state, nothing against the state."

In Russia they had similar issues with Stalin. We can say Lenin and Stalin were Communist because they placed economics in control of their 'State' government, but the implementation of laws and results were clearly Right-Wing Totalitarian. Russia, China, Italy, and Germany all lied about granting Marxist power to the people', by using democratic-anarchist worker controlled propaganda, but did not allow true Communism or Socialism. Stalin, Hitler, and Mussolini were all demagog liars were that used some Left-wing words to fool working-class people into believing that they would benefit under governments that would actually be Right-wing under their dictatorships. In Europe in the early 1900s you could not get much support from workers without using the word 'Social' in your platform, so yes politicians lied to get power. A true Left-wing leader will give up their military and political power voluntarily, after using it only in defense. General George Washington, our first president was a good example, although at times he certainly acted Right-wing during (executions) and after the Revolution (Farmer, Veteran, and Whiskey Rebellion).

No rational Left theories advocate perpetuating militant totalitarianism based on xenophobia or racism. Those themes of hateful legal violence are exclusively Right-wing. When State military violence against its own citizens occurs, it exposes which side leaders of parties are truly on. The more violence, the more Right-Wing the actions are by proof of theory. True progressive Left-wing leaders have been Gandhi, Martin Luther King, and Noam Chomsky; all of which advocated non-violence as a primary constant belief. The Left-wing leaders that deviate are considered less successful by history, because they competed using violence, which is vital to Right-wing theory.

*

Wealth Inequality

MIT Professor Noam Chomsky spoke on 'Wealth Inequality', as well as many other subjects. Chomsky believes inequality has been growing quite rapidly world-wide. Oxfam is a large agency that publishes on World Poverty & Inequality. In 2014 Oxfam reported that 90 individuals had half of World Wealth; In 2015 the number has been reduced to 62 individuals. The OECD (Organisation for Economic Co-operation and Development) reports that American poverty is worse than some 3rd World Countries, in some areas. We could end starvation in the World, the resources exist, but our economy is designed for all of that wealth to go to the extremely rich instead.

Chomsky gave a short talk on whether we could have a system without money. He said the question ignores the larger problem of modern tyranny, which happens to use money. We can have a different social order, if we did not have a tyrannical system which monopolizes all markets. "Giant Corporations are like totalitarian states." Power is going more and more into unaccountable institutions that distort markets.

Money is a tool, the problem is this network of private tyrannies (mega-companies) our founding fathers would have hated. Federal government is their enemy because it is large enough to threaten them, because the masses can influence it, and nothing else. Yes it does sound like Chomsky is advocating a conspiracy theory. He does not like to use the term 'conspiracy theory' because of the negative connotations. In one interview, he says "First of all, conspiracies like sub-urban developing to benefit oil companies exist." He says there are many conspiracies that we do not call theories because they are normal systemic workings where people get together in private and make plans they do not want to be public. Chomsky argues that some theories like 9/11 do not make logical sense to him, like "why would Bush blame Saudi Arabians for the plot if he wanted to attack Iraq?" It is an interesting point, but it is also odd Chomsky thinks the CIA was lock-step with Bush, with no other deep-state competitive operations, or rogue agents that may have gotten out of control. At least Chomsky has thought about and considered some possibilities, which is more than most people have done. I give him credit because he is current with much new information at his age, even if many departments got larger and more complex since the 1950s. More problems with his 9/11 assessment come to mind, like the CIA politics we have documented in many non-fiction library books regarding crazy non-sense plots that they conspired with Kennedy and Nixon about; which killed many people. Chomsky mentions some of these; but this book is on economics, so as a final note I will just say it is ironic the World Trade Center was an economic power.

Speaking of conspiracies, the 'less than 1%' are now led by 8 men. Eight men own the same wealth as the 3.6 billion people who make up the poorest half of humanity, according to a new report published by Oxfam. Had this new data been available last year, it would have shown that 9 billionaires owned the same wealth as the poorest half of the planet, and not 62, as Oxfam calculated at the time.

Oxfam's report, 'An economy for the 99 percent', shows that the gap between rich and poor is far greater than had been feared. It details how big business and the super-rich are fueling the inequality crisis by dodging taxes, driving down wages and using their power to influence politics. It calls for a fundamental change in the way we manage our economies so that they work for all people, and not just a fortunate few.

While Gates exemplifies how outsized wealth can be recycled to help the poor, Oxfam believes such "big philanthropy" is good, but does not address the fundamental problem. "Inequality matters and you cannot have a system where billionaires are systematically paying lower rates of tax than their secretary or cleaner," according to Reuters.

<u>These 8 Men own the same amount as the Poorest Half of the World's Wealth: 450 billion</u>
Bill Gates, Microsoft: $75 billion
Amancio Ortega, Fasion: $67 billion
Warren Buffett, Investor: $60.8 billion
Carlos Slim Helu, Telecom: $50 billion
Jeff Bezos, Amazon: $45.2 billion
Mark Zuckerberg, Facebook: $44.6 billion
Larry Ellison, CIA Oracle: $43.6 billion
Michael Bloomberg, Finance: $40 billion

The combined net worth of just Americans is estimated at $84.9 Trillion according to the federal reserve.

*

We must ease suffering for all at least;
End suffering for some at most.
*

Widow's Offering

Jesus sat down opposite the treasury where the offerings were put and watched the crowd putting their money into the Temple treasury. Many rich people threw in large amounts. But a poor widow came and put in two very small copper coins, worth only a few cents. Calling his disciples to him, Jesus said, "Truly I tell you, this poor widow has put more into the treasury than all the others. They all gave out of their wealth; but she, out of her poverty, put in everything—all she had to live on; her whole livelihood." - *Mark 12:41-44*

I am not usually one to quote the Bible, so I will give a disclaimer. According to this passage of text, Jesus did not himself donate to the Temple, nor did he seek to found a Temple, and reading the Bible may cause blindness. That being said, I include this quote to show how people who can barely pay their bills, do suffer more under a flat tax, than the rich who have an abundance in addition to the amount needed to pay their bills. It was challenging for me to understand the math, because the concept of a 'flat tax' sounds fair, but that is assuming everyone paying it has excess money in addition to all the bills needed for basic living.

Ironically the poor also tend to donate more, relative to what they have, than rich people; according to scientific studies. One reason is that poor people tend to be more empathetic, because they know what it means to go without. A sad result of this, is that they do not tend to save money, and so they stay poor. Some rich people may give more money than some poor people, but the reason they are rich is because they are taking wealth disproportionately to what individual people should have, if we are to share the planet more equally.

On NPR Paul Piff, a psychology researcher at the University of California, Berkeley, tells host Guy Raz about his studies; which show that poor people are actually more charitable than the rich.

The article also included this note to be fair to some rich people: "40 billionaires announced this past week that they'll give at least half their fortunes to charity. Bill Gates and Warren Buffett unveiled the list, which also includes Larry Ellison, Mayor Michael Bloomberg and George Lucas. The total promise so far: $125 billion."

*

Prison industrial complex in America is out of control. Mass incarceration affects millions of citizens, by taking away their rights, and draining tax money. Lower-class citizens get charged with drug charges, which is really a health-care issue.

*

Reality: Fact and Fiction

In Chomsky's view, truth about political-economic realities is systemically distorted or suppressed by elite corporate business and propaganda. Corporations use our public media, advertising, and think-tanks to promote their own interests. Chomsky's books and lectures reveal corruption and the underlying ideological truth behind political-economic systems.

Chomsky believes that "common sense" is all that is required to see through webs of illusion, and see the truth. Common sense needs some consciousness which is able to ask questions, and find answers. Awareness and critical investigation can be used by average people, to solve every-day problems at home, at work, or in society. Chomsky accepts moral intellectual responsibility to deal with world problems, but admits many others are unethical in exchange for economic survival or rewards. Chomsky says free democracy is also a worthy goal.

111

"I am not a committed pacifist. I would not hold that it is under all imaginable circumstances wrong to use violence, even though use of violence is in some sense unjust. I believe that one has to estimate relative justices. But the use of violence and the creation of some degree of injustice can only be justified on the basis of the claim and the assessment-which always ought to be undertaken very, very seriously and with a good deal of skepticism that this violence is being exercised because a more just result is going to be achieved." - *Noam Chomsky*

Liberal non-violence is not as weak a position as war-hawks tend to portray it. Non-violent resistance to authoritarianism is different than extreme pure Pacifism. The best Left-wing leaders often make the distinction that they want to minimize violence, but self-defense can be justified as a rare exception to the rule, rather than a cause for frequent preemptive attacks. The main Left-wing tool is compassionate negotiation, and when that fails we use sanctions and 'restraining orders'. The critique by the Right of this Left-wing peaceful tactic, is that peace allows Right-wing war-hawks to continue arming for war (Chamberlain's failure to control Hitler's aggression before WW2). This is of course the catch-22 problem of war justification, as I explained with diagrams in Operation 10 COW. It takes strong compassionate humanitarian leaders for societies to break out of the self-destructive war-monger paradigm. We rarely see Left-wing volunteers glorified because they are not financed by capital for obvious reasons; the main reason being that plutocrats who have most of the World's wealth, and got most of their money from being part of the Military Industrial Complex (MIC) because it includes the largest corporations, now provides the funding for all major political leaders and propaganda on commercial media outlets.

Our government run by corporations seems to be playing 'bad cop / good cop' with us; Bait and switch, give us the worst, then make us beg for the less worse. If we are not being with nature more than destroying it, we have to balance our system better. as an architect, i learned how our built environment could be more integrated with nature, and still achieve progress in technologies. I was largely unable to find enough clients to pursue those goals, and was black-listed because of my environmental dedication. We must practice where-ever we are allowed to work on our own designs.

A major SCOD argument is that Totalitarian rule using our military to oppress our own citizens is wrong. Military force is never really Left-wing, and any liberal that does use violent aggression is using Right-wing tactics. I base what I am saying on Left-wing theory and the practice of those leaders like Mandela, and yes the ones that were not elected officials but still have incredible popularity and social influence. All the way back to the French Revolution, the failures on the Left were always due to using violence which contradicted the main values they were fighting for, so the Left realized that Pacifism was part of the humanitarian core of their ideology; as opposed to the Right. I also think that good and bad ways of practicing Communism or Capitalism should be discussed when labeling leaders 'Right or Left', as corruption at the top levels never seems to allow the systems to work well. Yes I agree Bernie Sanders is one of the best leaders we have.

The reason I mention this semantic issue at all, is because i Right-wing people call dictators Left-wing simply because the dictator lied or fought to implement Left-wing politics, but to get power or once they got in power they acted Right-wing overall. I think a better way to look at that is like Sauron's ring, absolute power corrupts absolutely, and cannot make for Left-wing values. Right-wing values have to do with individual 'might is right' dog-eat-dog trickle-down oligarchy.

I do realize that I am using my own progressive SCOD interpretation. Most people focus on 'state' vs 'free-market'; rather than 'humanitarian democracy' vs 'corporate dictatorships' which is how I interpret political theory differences.

Political parties are interesting as a sociological experiment. Libertarian Socialism is basically an advanced Anarchy where once there was no government, but then a free society of individuals develops that can practice direct democracy, voluntary socialism, and cooperate organically.

One way to avoid bad leaders, is for us all to find common ground in as many social conventions as possible that represent us directly. We have come a long way from the French Revolution, and liberals now desire peaceful change on mass by social means. Bernie Sanders may be the best representative for true Left-wing politics we have today. No one on the Right seems to come close to representing civil rights of individuals to be able to survive, and our community rights to preserve clean public water, land, and air. If we do not remind ourselves of the past, we will be doomed to make similar mistakes.

*

Excerpts from Chomsky's 1970 speech 'Future Government':

"I think it is useful to set up as a framework for discussion four somewhat idealized positions with regard to the role of the state in an advanced industrial society. I want to call these positions: (1) classical liberal, (2) libertarian socialist, (3) state socialist, (4) state capitalist, and I want to consider each in turn. Also, I'd like to make clear my own point of view in advance, so that you can evaluate and judge what I am saying. I think that the libertarian socialist concepts, and by that I mean a range of thinking that extends from left-wing Marxism through to anarchism, I think that these are fundamentally correct and that they are the proper and natural extension of classical liberalism into the era of advanced industrial society."

114

"In contrast, it seems to me that the ideology of state socialism, i.e. what has become of Bolshevism, and that of state capitalism, the modern welfare state, these of course are dominant in the industrial societies, but I believe that they are regressive and highly inadequate social theories, and a large number of our really fundamental problems stem from a kind of incompatibility and inappropriateness of these social forms to a modern industrial society.

"If we were to withdraw the consent of the governed, as I think we should, we are withdrawing our consent to have these men and the interests they represent, govern and manage American society and impose their concept of world order and their criteria for legitimate political and economic development in much of the world. Although an immense effort of propaganda and mystification is carried on to conceal these facts, nonetheless facts they remain.

"We have today the technical and material resources to meet man's animal needs. We have not developed the cultural and moral resources or the democratic forms of social organization that make possible the humane and rational use of our material wealth and power.

"Conceivably, the classical liberal ideals, as expressed and developed in their libertarian socialist form, are achievable. But if so, only by a popular revolutionary movement, rooted in wide strata of the population, and committed to the elimination of repressive and authoritarian institutions, state and private. To create such a movement is the challenge we face and must meet if there is to be an escape from contemporary barbarism."

- Noam Chomsky

*

For those that don't think politics affects them, the premise of government is to represent the will of THE PEOPLE, not Commercial Corporations or a War-addicted Military (which is the way it is now). If we feel it is not working correctly for us, we need to change it.

115

People who have jobs or pensions under the party rulers, we can perhaps excuse their opinions; the rest of us might want some real ability to live our lives. Hopefully in the future people will be able to admit that Corporate MIC America was a schizophrenic system from the start, doomed because it was headed in a totalitarian direction (much like Russia and Germany around WW2, what a funny coincidence).

Many of us realize there is a problem when we experience Loss of Freedom and ability to pay bills regardless of how excellent our skills, intelligence, education, or work; or in many cases BECAUSE our qualities are too competitive for those in power. The idea that everyone can "make it' if only they try harder, and are willing to hurt enough other people in the process in order to keep them from getting your profits (just so long as your family is provide for)", is fucking insane in a "civilized society", and yet that is our dominant ideology.

A profit driven system rewards greed if you can get away with it by paying those that share power enough, and tricking everyone else outside your family into thinking "if only they can work as hard as you, some day they may be worthy to have what you have". To have a system that makes individuals at war with each-other for survival, to keep the masses constantly divided on what is "THE TRUTH", really is the 1984 nightmare that George Orwell told us we should resist at all costs. For most of us it means we must always try to 'win' by cheating better in our businesses, while convincing people it is in their interest to let us win, or to make it seem like we are all benefiting equally; and for others it means they go homeless, starve, and die early.

*

Open letter to Plutocrats: We have a Neo-Nazi KKK associated regime running our country. I am a child of a patriotic family, from generations of patriotic Americans. As a child I marched around the town band-stand on the 4th of July waving the American flag. We celebrated the American Revolution, because we valued our American Freedoms. To me those freedoms include free speech, freedom to practice any religion you want, freedom to adopt any cultural or fashion styles that you want, and freedom to over throw Nazis, tyrants, and oligarchies that threaten democratic freedom any-where, meaning not just abroad, but at home too. I also learned about 'propaganda' in college, and because I could not earn a living with that degree, I joined the military and became a veteran. MIC Corporate puppet-politicians, you are all on notice shit-for-brains, for bringing us to this point. Remember, remember, to stay positive when people come knocking on palace doors. Slanche' suckers (that means cheers)! - *Drogo*

I am excited that more Americans are catching up with things some of us had figured out about our beloved country years ago.

The more we learn about how big business works, the more we realize they have usually stolen from other producers and copied other artists in many ways. Most realistic art seems to be based on 'cheating' or copying; using techniques to transfer the illusion. Which person has contributed more to society to deserve more money than thousands of people in the World have? We must realize the answer is "no one can earn a hoard".

I study and make reports when on sabbatical vacation with no living wage income: NSA Body of Secrets, CIA Legacy of Ashes, CIA Dulles Devil's Chessboard, FBI Bureau, CIA Secret History; these are NON-FICTION books. Devil's Chessboard (CIA): about an upper-class German conservative who disliked the Nazis as Hitler rose to power, but - "In order to keep his position at the mining firm, he had been forced to join the Nazi-run German Labor Front."

*

Conspiracy theories as valid patterns for study. I think some people base their reality on what they want their emotions to be, more than any 'facts' might dictate. So people that want to be happy, ignore theories or things that would make them sad; and vise-versa; when I talk with people that work with theories similar to my own about existence, I feel sane, but when I talk to people that think all theories are 'crazy conspiracy theories' I feel like something is wrong with me. We have been made to think that 'conspiracies' and 'theories' are things that are not real by the 2-party corporate political media system. Any deviations from that duality / polarity programming, are met by party-line propaganda in society that creates a desire to push you away and label you a 'nut' or worse. Tiger-swan military mercenaries labeled Standing-Rock protesters as "insurgent" terrorists, in their official papers, as reported by the Intercept.

Our main problem is a system that makes money for only a few by polluting, imprisoning, and killing the rest of us. Hint: It is not the EPA, NPS, or Schools doing most of that; and yes i know the military recycles, and some companies are "green". Terrorism and Addiction are ideological socio-psychological symptoms of deeper systemic problems that require loving education, thriving communities, and police action, not wars. The way our government and corporations work at the highest levels, is destructive to Life on the Planet.

We have put power in the hands of ruthless tyrants and greedy desperadoes, instead of loving caretakers and peaceful healers. Exploitation of workers who usually work harder at least physically than their bosses, and wasting and hoarding wealth and resources that should belong to everyone (if anyone at all) should be criminal.

Political-economic power should be given to loving caretakers and peaceful healers.

If we resist corruption, or do not fit in as a slave, we are told we cannot even have shelter or food. There is a GREEN PEACE and LOVE revolution that is not being 'televised' in the main-stream; but it is built on people power unity of the masses. Hackers help the masses with international revolution, information, communication, boycotts, protests, art, films, propaganda, and then laws (as lawyers and politicians catch up). I might make a better wage-slave, if there were a job that I was fit for; with less pollution, incarceration, and violent threats involved; and more nature, freedom, and peaceful goodwill.

Bombs and guns are not the way of progress. Destroying our ability to sustain ourselves on Earth is not the way of true progress. All the 'War on Terror' violence just feeds violence, on both sides. To use guns and bombs on either side is stupid ultimately, since TERROR is an ideology fueled by ideologies, and to use terror perpetuates it since violence is terrible, and the effects cause the desire for more terror, no matter how many are killed, there are always those that desire to resist oppression. The more extreme their need for survival, the more extreme their tactics will be. Aldous Huxley understood this, and there are many issues besides violence we need to address in this Brave New World. Power matters, we need to take the power back for the people economically, and in all ways.

*

119

The 'We Stand United NYC Rally' summoned the Resistance Comedy Army, using the internet across the globe. Comedy is going to keep social pressure on authority until leaders figure out how to actually drain the swamp, and who are suitable replacements to represent the population. If people could vote more on local and national issues, we could save many lives with more social workers that include employment or life therapists able to get people what they need to live.

Political Party leaders funded by corporations, are owned by corporations. Democrats bribed news outlets to only pit Hillary against Trump, because the party heads were sure she could beat him. That is the main reason that Bernie Sanders was not given much media attention during the race; and also ironically why Bernie would have beat Trump, if Hillary voters had voted for Bernie, because Bernie draws from the far Right and Left.

The history of the WV Coal Mine Wars was similar to what is happening with Federal Government currently. The companies behind the corporate 2-parties are just pitting us against each other to serve their mutual billionaire goals. Both need to go.

*

Compassionate People Power = Humanitarian Society

Nina Turner on Success:
"3 bones: wish bone, jaw bone, back bone;
finite disappointment, but infinite hope."

*

Capitalism should transform from within companies. Democratic and anarchist cooperatives need to take over the system. Only when we can spot power-hungry leaders, will we remove crony capitalists from most of democracy.

The elites that rule America, have been playing a shell game with our minds through propaganda. To break their power over us, ignoring them and continuing with our lives as though they don't exist, does not work; as we will continue to serve them by existing within their system which fuels them. To break their power, we need to know who they are, and how to empower the masses more; which not only includes economics, but also education and wisdom of communal compassion which does not allow for tyrants.

*

SCOD is studying the art of space and time between people in community, and working with disabled artists. Everyone has unique needs in addition to common basic needs. Go Green!

GREEN Party policies:
Curb costly sprawl development by helping more counties create smart, sustainable plans to guide future growth; Stop rollbacks on laws that protect our waters from pollution created by development; Ensure new renewable energy facilities are sited to both protect our agricultural land and make it easier to generate more renewable energy; and Protect our transportation wins that increase accountability from repeal and vetoes.

Democracy does not mean lesser of two evils, it means providing the means for citizens to vote for issues that they feel represent them, otherwise they will not bother to vote because voting becomes meaningless. Masses of disenfranchised voters means there is something wrong with a system that is not functioning democratically.

If you are doing ok with what you have, and taking steps towards what you want, you are good. We must continue to do what we can using joy, knowledge, and love; wisdom comes with the experience of those ingredients.

SCOD Environmental Design Philosophy

Eco-villages: Bio-diverse communities that design, build, inhabit, maintain, and develop environmental architecture and ways of life; Eco-villages fit into SCOD Amalgams.

Amalgams: Combine collages of SCOD Ecovillage master plans, designed for manifesting in phases over time; Amalgams fit into SCOD Matrix.

SCOD Matrix: Total SCOD Master Plan; includes all literature, art, and amalgams. Urban Amalgams have high populations, Rural have low populations; both focus on Green Space.

SCOD Designs - often must modify existing architecture, in order to serve the new ecological-collective networks which extend into various communities. Homesteads become Nature Centers - to preserve the natural environment for maximum acres of hunting and gathering, with minimal impact housing and trading. Economics becomes subservient to Government based on environmental stewardship for harmonious co-habitation with renewable energy resources.

Land - it is vital that the organic nature of sites be preserved.

Urban Amalgams - high population to green space ratio, Hives often act as county council centers

Rural Amalgams - low population to green space ratio, Eco-villages surrounded by wilderness

*

American libertarians tend to say they want less government, but what that would mean in current reality is that corporations would have total control with no democracy worth a damn. Free markets are not possible with unrestrained mega-corporations monopolizing the Nation's wealth; state capitalism without representation for the workers and those unable to work for the available companies, is the equivalent of a totalitarian state where only consuming or boycotting would have any influence, until the lobbyists made that illegal. Removing subsidies would not solve those larger problems, it would only rearrange some of the monopolies; unless there are some missing study models.

In our current system, if people think 'State Capitalism' is worth keeping, and population keeps growing, health care should be a right. Less government would be possible if the system and population would allow people to live free on our own land. The poor are getting poorer with less jobs available, because the plutocracy is draining and polluting all our resources. If people think our government should not use our own tax money to help us, then the whole system needs to be dismantled, and rebuilt as a real democracy. I will not bother arguing against others on this point, unless there would be a benefit from it, but I will publish my opinion. I will also defend my right to have an opinion.

Tarp money and Wall-Street bail-outs were bullshit!

"For almost 50 years, the US economy and society has taken a great leap backward, accelerating during the past 3 presidencies. Not only have we experienced the reversal of past socio-economic legislation, but also our presidents and Congress have dragged us into multiple aggressive wars." - *Dr. James Petras*

Those that think it is unpatriotic to criticize our own oligarch leaders, do not understand patriotic responsibility. It is our responsibility as citizens to tell our leaders what we want in a democracy, not to just obey like under a monarchy. It is fair to be responsible for our own government, if we pay taxes, and are citizens.

*

Futurist Philosophy

We plan for the future, for our children's inheritance!

Apology To The Children of the Future,

I am sorry that we of Generation X have not done more to preserve our Nature Environment. Yes we participated in protests, and various activist roles, but we have been largely apathetic as a whole, and the grip that the Baby-Boomer Generation has had on government has not lessened. Their corporate corruption certainly set the stage for Trump and his ilk. There was rumor among our revolutionaries of assassinating all the demagogues, but that did not seem reasonable to do on a weekend, without a viable replacement system.

Instead of acting on our angst and over-throwing the system in order to replace with with real democracy, we instead spent our money (what little we could make in a diminishing economy) on movies and video games, preparing the way for Millennials. Apathy, ignorance, greed, and arrogance are to blame for the pollution of our water, land, and air. I honestly thought that Rambo and Commando would solve all our problems, by kicking the ass of every enemy. Well we certainly helped accomplish global destruction of nature, terror torture, and murder; through our aggression and belligerence. The shells of wasted ammo piled high, and the smog from spent fuel hangs heavy in the air. The smell of burning oil wells is our generation's new 'napalm in the morning'.

Cities have poisoned their own water supplies, corporations have waged wars on workers, and yet we still allow terrible, evil people to control our lives and ruin your future. I am sorry my children, I would have liked to have more green spaces for you to enjoy for quality of life, and technology for you to use for renewable energy. And yet we are developing every square foot of our country by paving over it, and building wasteful architecture. I have quite serving that system, to the best of my ability, and I fight against it, peacefully as much as I can. For us, I pledge I will never stop the struggle to allow us to thrive with nature, responsibly, and most of all for you because I love you.
- Drogo Empedocles

*

"We are all energy vibrations and reality exists where most of the fluctuations in energy overlap creating constructive interference. we are the result of a universe that is attempting to exist, to settle into stability." *- Beamer*

The value we pay or place on things is often very arbitrary. Economics is artificial, but psychologically substantial. Economies depend on variable trader speculation, and which commodities are offered in supply or demand.

How can we live doing more of what we enjoy? What aspects of society can allow more of that freedom. This book has some suggestions, but it is up to us whether we ask questions, seek answers to those questions, and then act on the answers.

It is easier for me to handle debates in person or on the phone, but online is much harder to see the font, and comprehend intent in semantics. When an ego-driven person calls me egotistical, the debate becomes finger pointing "You are wrong; no you!". I don't really enjoy fighting that much anymore, but I am a fighter and will defend my ability to express myself in some ways.

For as much anger and hatred appears online, the internet is connecting people from around the world, with common interests and feelings; wishing to be neighbors. Another book might address social dynamics more than this one has. We are all neighbors in some sense, at our home we call Earth; even travelers stop over, visit, and stay the night somewhere.

A friend of mine commented "Same shit different year." Another friend said "If the rich were not in power, it would be someone else, perhaps worse." To which I have to say "Yes, but the scale of wealth inequality has worsened in recent decades, where as we were more egalitarian with our wealth distribution, charts have reversed and more closely resembles Rome at its height or the aristocracy before the French Revolution again." That is considered a fact according to the Piketty research. America was more egalitarian from 1940-1980 in the past century, before our recent regression regarding income distribution. That was the age of Franklin Roosevelt's New Deal economics. We can be in part responsible for a 'New GREEN Deal'; we can call it whatever we want.

The thesis of journalist Paul Mason's book <u>Post-Capitalism</u>, is that new technologies (computers, internet, cell phones, and associated developments), have caused the decline of Capitalism; which is likely to be replaced within a few decades by an entirely new socio-economic system; 'Post-Capitalism'. Note: all new movements are post-modern, until that era's 'modern' gets named, and the 'post' response gets an appropriate corresponding title too, by historians.

Writing a book on economics may be a bad investment. There are many ways to think about ways to live. We can ask ourselves what economics has to do with ways of living. Funny questions like that, keep me amused endlessly.

*

95 Million Americans Not Employed

95,055,000 Americans have no employer-job income in 2016! For some reason, the public media 'Unemployment Reports' from the US Department of Labor are not listing the largest and most important number. According to their own data charts (which do not copy well as a direct link for specific info, perhaps on purpose) the Bureau of Labor Statistics 'Household Data' Table A-1; in November 2016 there were over 95 Million Americans 'not employed' total. To clarify, over 95,000,000 adults have no 'outside-the-family-home' income (using the 'not in the labor force' chart). Many adult workers have no formal income in America. Over 38 million men and almost 57 million women, of those jobless are adults over the age of 16 (using the seasonally adjusted charts).

The total population of the USA is 324,954,000. The US civilian population of adult citizens between the ages of 15-65 is apx. 206,189,000 (male + female) [Wikipedia]; of those 152 million are 'employed' (includes over 7 million unemployed), and 95 million are not included. About 152 million employees are having to support 95 million other adults of all ages AND all the 62 million children. Although we have men and women working formal or informal paying or volunteer jobs, the ratio of income is perhaps about the same as before Equal Rights (152/157). Worse yet the economy shows no signs of improving, and based on the facts appears to be getting worse every year (accounting for inflation ratios).

There is a pattern trend in relation to the number of years (from 1975-2016) and the unemployed numbers (58 million to 95 million). In 1975 the total 'jobless population' was 58,627,000 (over 16 years of age). So since 1975 the ratio of population to non-employed has at least doubled. Our total population has grown in that time (1975-2016) only a little over 100 million more; therefore the disproportionate numbers means that although the total population only grew by 1/3, the jobless population grew by 1/2. 'Fact-checkers' claim numbers not included (people in school or elderly over 65) reduce 95 million to 20 million, but I am not convinced and have not yet verified their numbers [Politifact]. I believe counting students over 16 as potential PAID labor force is fair (as they should not be slaves), so if we subtract 40 million elders (population over 65 not verified) that still leaves 55 million adults with no official income that should be getting a living wage if we believe that people have a right to life.

This data makes a parabola chart showing perpetual rapid job loss by the millions within decades. In one generation the masses could all be slaves to corporate plutocracy, with no ability to vote on anything except American Idol, will own less and less property, and will become more impoverished with each generation. One conclusion could be that we are indeed long overdue for major reform, we have been misled by our leaders, and real revolution is needed. The Green Party, SCOD, and others are by necessity already exploring alternative grass-roots economies. We should also break up the Federal government into smaller sections of states (by time-zones), each with democratic directly elected presidential councils. The system trend resembles a plutocracy that keeps the masses enslaved only to benefit the wealthy elites.

*

On the Process of Belief

Faith by definition is not scientific, but Belief in science is real when the evidence is shown and believed, and the purpose is considered worthy. Trustworthy belief is not the same as blind faith; it just means we believe that unseen forces like gravity exist because we feel the effects and accept the proof, and we might also take the word of others who have conducted experiments. That type of rational scientific belief is dependent on social coercion, not just personal opinion based on observation, just as much as the worst aspects of religions were dependent on social acceptance of the 'truth' by neighbors and authorities; for better or worse.

Egalitarian Economics

Economics is a belief based philosophy that we can use psychology (behavioral) and accounting (math) to facilitate successful transactions of commerce. Some people want rational and peaceful economic systems in harmony with nature, and others want predatory 'winner takes all' systems as over-bearing master abusers. Before Marx wrote about communism and socialism, Christianity was founded on communal living and social services (similar to tribal Pagans). Christians social services are based on the concept that 'giving is its own reward' because God loves them, wants them to give without material or monetary benefit, and will reward them in the after-life for their sacrifice. AA (Alcoholics Anonymous) uses a Christian prohibitionist type of addiction therapy, run on member based donations and volunteer work. Buddhism has a similar charity concept that encourages vows of poverty and sacrifice.

Rather than predatory State Capitalism, or dogmatic Church Monarchy, we could change towards more moral humane systems. We can reward 'givers' more than 'takers'. We need to be aware that poor give more away freely, and the rich take more than their fair share; because the system currently works in reverse. So we can develop a middle-ground between the two extremes of Religion and Business ideology.

Communism clearly has the modesty of religious morality, and Socialism has the best aspects of trade & barter ethics. The best type of Capitalism will embrace egalitarianism for the majority of the population, that makes more property public and rewards those that give to others the most.

Predatory Capitalism is like an addiction, it is very hard to break a harmful habit if we feel we cannot stop ourselves from doing, even when it hurts ourselves and others more than it benefits them. Therefore perhaps a SCOD system of economic transition can be similar to AA, where we can admit we have a problem, and that by helping others we are solving the problem. Then we can begin apologizing to all those we could have given more to, when we only practiced Capitalism.

Biological Sciences and Liberal Arts must change Business into a socio-ecological economy. Redefining what is 'WEALTH' and what makes it desirable, is changing the psychology of economics. Wealth of mind and economy has more to do with basic needs, and the ability to transact socially for happiness, than collecting coins (if the term is worth anything). We are doing this step-by-step, day-by-day; with kindness, compassion, and considerate knowledge that can admit the limits of science to measure happiness or pain, and the limits of economics to value human life or any life. Tipping progress away from superficial capital gain, towards the wealth of our society and ecology, is the only way to go if we want to have a better world community.

Green American Dream

Being GREEN in industry or as a consumer is not enough, if most have no reasonable liberty because they can barely meet their survival basics. A Green Economy should meet the health basics of all citizens, allowing us our share of 'civil rights' for control over our own lives within a system that can balance despite democratic deviations, and help us find a willing place in a desired community, unit, or homestead to be successful. This dream can be available to all, not just a minority.

Even if the US system collapses, this is how SCOD communities should regard trade and barter on the local level, always. A conscious majority, will consider minority independent rights; and can be persuaded to stop by protest; and course correct or shut-down system expansion. No corporate tyranny should ruin the lives of smaller less-powerful groups. One person protesting is enough to reassess any action by holistic council and vote.

130

The market is flooded with artisan crafts, so most cannot find a venue to sustain income; however some are able to make some money online or at events. Supply and demand must be environmentally reconsidered in sustainable terms that allow flexible adaptability in accord with changing mortal lives. As long as one person in a community is getting some income, there will be social pressure for distribution, and so there can be hope of survival in between periods of depression.

The spiral of history cycles through similar economic periods. Patterns of power do repeat in various amalgams. We cannot predict what will precisely happen, but civilization has made progress towards better qualities of living for all, because enough people have cared to make some improvements.

I am sure conservative professional economists will not like this book. Many people are not interested in science or art, conspiracies or theories; and some think they know more than anyone else. Within the reality of our system, we are lucky to have partners that love us, when the bills come due. Thank all those that help us to live, and to critics: "Shalom, it's a poem" (make it rhyme at bargain prices).

Paying artists to live and express themselves, helps them to be functional in society. Then maybe artists might respect critical opinions more, in a system that demands conformance. SCOD work is for those of us who believe in mutual compassion, science, and art, and can be interested in differences as much as similarities. Thank you for your support. To transform our Capitalist system, basic living needs for every citizen must be met through generous egalitarian Socialism, before any future Anarchist Libertarian Communist Utopia can be manifested sustainably for the masses.

I would love to have a chance to employ tons of people, but our current economic system feels that even life has no value, because environment, ethical, love, and peace based projects

131

have no financial return. How many total factors contribute to systemic apathy and victim and prey scenarios? I cannot calculate as well as others; but greed, pride, and ignorance could be identified as social problems by common sense, not just other professionals in sustainability. Perhaps those factors are human nature, or perhaps a more nurturing system would help solve those problems, who knows? I do believe that if we give more of our money to loving people, who are happy to give to others, then our economy will do what it is supposed to do; which is to perpetually redistribute a monetary supply of material symbols that represent cultural and personal value attached to goods, services, and commodities which are tangible and intangible.

In a SCOD Economy

Distributive wealth value literally determines a rich person, by economic vote; like how Spanish workers in Mondragon vote on their bosses from within the socialist cooperative company; but with direct money, given to the one who redistributes fairly.

My own wealth value in a distributive democracy would be minimal or moderate at best, as I prefer privacy. I would not be elected to be a rich leader in such a society, because I would not want much more power and responsibility than I could handle, if ambition is in proportion to desire, I would be lucky to have my basic needs met, and movie night. To me the problem of politics is best seen as Tolkien's one Ring metaphor of what we should do with ultimate power positions of power; as Plato realized about Socrates, the ones that would do the best job, are often the very ones that do not want power for long periods.

Bad people make better bosses than good people, if boss means a bully leader for an oligarchy. Good people make better leaders, if a 'good leader' means a knowledgeable and wise distributive decision maker who wields power in favor of equal rights, peace, and love. Money must correspond with community.

132

Corporate crony politics is not legitimate, it is corrupted against truths we hold to be self-evident; such as our natural human rights of "life, liberty, and the pursuit of happiness"*. SCOD organic economic systems in amalgams will be founded on our natural human rights for all people.

see American Declaration of Independence

* End Book *

**

Resources:

Oxfam's 2017 report, - *'An economy for the 99 percent'*, "8 Men own the same wealth as the poorest half of the world." A friend of mine added up the numbers: "I don't understand, that only comes to 450 billion, the combined net worth just of Americans is estimated at 84.9 trillion according to the federal reserve. What am I missing? " Good question, I said. It is because Oxfam meant the poorest half of the world's population's wealth, not total world wealth.

J is for Junk Economics ; Killing the Host, How Financial Parasites and Debt Destroy Global Economics - books by **Michael Hudson**

Dr. Dean Baker co-founded CEPR in 1999. His areas of research include housing and macroeconomics, intellectual property, Social Security, Medicare and European labor markets. He is the author of several books, including; Rigged: How Globalization and the Rules of the Modern Economy Were Structured to Make the Rich Richer. His blog, "Beat the Press," provides commentary on economic reporting. He received his B.A. from Swarthmore College and his Ph.D. in Economics from the University of Michigan.

Atlantic magazine online; **Thomas Piketty**
Opensecrets.org; Center for Responsive Politics
1101 14th St., NW; Suite 1030; Washington, DC

Professor Mark Blyth, Youtube videos
"In 2015, after the Bailouts $28 billion went to Wall Street BONUSES (not earnings, b-o-n-u-s-e-s), and $14 billion total went to all minimum wage workers in America." - Economist Blyth

Richard D. Wolff, Youtube videos - "Capitalism 101";
"When and Why will Capitalism end?"

Economist Thomas Piketty R>G

Return on Capital (R) is greater than the over-all growth of the economy (G). It does not matter how smart or productive you are, wealth will go more to those already rich in general. Piketty calls this a central contradiction of Capitalism. This Law of Capital reinforces wealth inequality. Old ‚wealth can diminish, and new wealth is generated, but those are exceptions which nullify each-other statistically. Most of the population will be subject to the whims of the already rich, and will never become rich no matter how good, productive, or ambitious they behave.

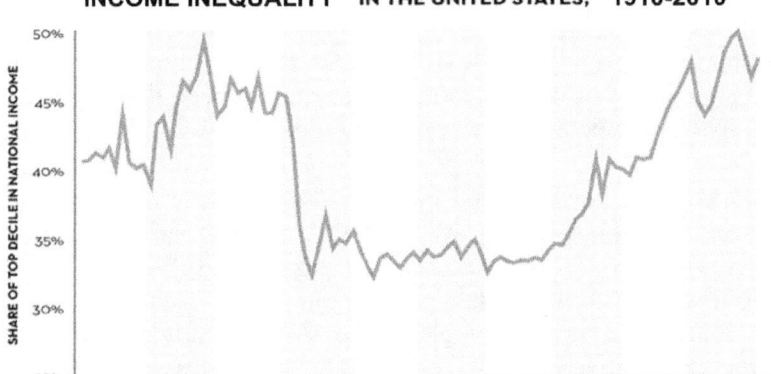

INCOME INEQUALITY IN THE UNITED STATES, 1910-2010

Thomas Piketty - Economic Chart shows shares to **Top 10%** of population

This chart shows 'Income Inequality' with most of the National Income going to only 10% of the population. Piketty says that total 'WEALTH' inequality is greater than income inequality (not shown here). However this chart is symbolic of the overall challenges we face regarding systemic power flow; and thus as an artist interpreting economic prophets, I invite you to use your own investigative skills, and poetic language, to explore more charts that I will not bore my readers with further here.

Business Mirror Magazine

"It is quite obvious that progress is linked to the health of our environment. We can't keep on talking about economic development while we ignore the pressing problems related to environment protection. There is also a sense of urgency; the sooner we address these issues, the better for everyone."
- Rojas in his article 'Environment and Our Economy'

Outdoor Festivals for Preservation
Musical movie 'The Sound of Music' - "The sound of music helps keep hills alive!" - SCOD slogan for outdoor concerts to preserve wild landscapes

<u>Deschooling Society</u>, 1971 by **Ivan Illich** - counterproductivity: when institutions of modern industrial society impede their purported aims; specific diseconomy; conviviality tools vs machines

S.C.O.D. is the 'Sustainable Cooperative for Organic Development', a grass-roots non-profit educational, design, and publishing group. Lower-case 'scod' can be used to express sub-genres of the environmental movement, perma-culture, bio-design, history, education, and alternative architecture that resemble SCOD Thesis criteria (alternative utopian concepts). SCOD uses philosophical theory to practice art work for clients, communities, and provide public education. SCOD's main focus has been to research, design, communicate, and support organic individuals, homesteads, villages, cooperatives, and world-wide networks.

Robin Hood - The wolf's-head economic theory is a sub-utopian under-ground system for rebels and thieves who "steal from the rich, to give to the poor" within a dystopian oppressive totalitarian government. Outlaws can represent the masses, if they give generously back to those who help to conceal them, and freely give charity hand-outs to those suffering the most.

Bibliography:

Assault On Reason; Gore, Al; Penguin Books 2008

The Golden Rule; Wattles, Jeffrey; Oxford University Press, 1996

Quotes from the Dalai Lama; (English); **Dalai Lama**; Gee, Margaret; Andrews McMeel Publishing 2001

Groundwork of the Metaphysics of Morals; Critique of Practical Reason; **Immanuel Kant**; Cambridge University Press 1997

The Ideal of a Rational Morality; GM Singer; Oxford 2002; p270

'Towards a Global Ethic' (An Initial Declaration); urbandharma.org

Rock Wheeler of National Geographic; Theory talks

Jesus of History; Zanzig, Thomas; Saint Mary's Press 1992

J is for Junk Economics, book by **Michael Hudson**

The Way of the **Peaceful Warrior**: A Book That Changes Lives; Millman, Dan; 2000; H.J. Kramer with New World Library, CA

When Miners March: The Story of the **WV Coal Miners**; Blizzard, William C.; 2004

Complete Book of Zen; Kit, Wong Kiew; 1998 Element Book Inc.

An Inconvenient Truth: The Planetary Emergency of Global Warming and What We Can Do About It; Gore, Al; 2006 Rodale

Ancient Civilizations; Scarre & Fagan; 1997 Lindbriar & Longman

Blackwater: Rise of the World's Most Powerful Mercenary Army; Scahill, Jeremy; 2007 Nation Books

Mondragon Corporation Cooperative, Spain - workers vote on bosses

Yanis Varoufakis - Greek Economist & Finance Minister

[Using Libraries, Google, Wikipedia, & DoD Website]

News Media Sources: NPR, PBS, NBC, CBS, Jimmy Dore, Young Turks, Washington Post, NY Times, Democracy Now, etc...

The next mass extinction is already underway, billions of various species have died recently due to human over-consumption/population "Population extinctions today are orders of magnitude more frequent than species extinctions. Population extinctions, however, are a prelude to species extinctions, so Earth's sixth mass extinction episode has proceeded further than most assume. 50% of the number of animal individuals that once shared Earth with us are already gone, as are billions of populations." Scientists determined the human causes for biological annihilation were largely due to rich industrialists, and concluded economically and ecologically that we will all pay the price. Species percentages were determined by surveys from 1900–2015. - *Proceedings of the National Academy of Sciences (PNAS report published 7/10-/2017)*

Contributors:
Friends who made me feel wealthy:
Aeyla of the Hill People, Noel Tavano, Polly MacDavid,
Stephen Parnes, Ragos, Harrison, Beamer, Tammi, Tammy,
Rhonda, Nina, Nena, Tom & Jenny, Michael Shor, Joe Zappa,
Cheri Morris, Kim Woods, Wim Verveen, Pat Long, Omi,
Sama, Phyllis Grant, Dulce, Curie,
and other SCOD associates
Thank you all!!!

This book is dedicated to Odd Fellow Brian King
* RIP Brian King FLT *
**

Books Produced by Drogo Empedocles

MOSS: My Old School Short-Stories (Compendium)
Stories of Fiction, Fantasy, and Adventure (Action)
Tales of Amazing Magic and Science
SOS V1: GIFS; SOS V2: SOG; SOS V3: SASS
Medieval Fantasy Stories; Science Fiction Stories
*

Pitcher of Immortality - Byzantine Role-playing
Multiple Choice Adventures
Harpers Ferry Houses
Harpers Faery Magic Bible
Hopper's Furry Tale
SCOD: Sustainable Cooperative for Organic Development Thesis
Operation 10 COW: Ten Conscientious Objections to War
BDU: Boot-Camp Diary Unauthorized
Art Beyond Reality: Portfolio of Walton Stowell
Dreams Precede Reality: Art by Nena Stowell
Architectural Art: Artography of Kip Stowell
BOG Peeps: Beautiful Organic Garden People
WAY TOO MUCH: Successful Living
SCOD Economics
*

Blackberry Cove Herbal: Traditional Appalachian Herbalism -
Linda Rago
- Wear A Spring of Thyme: Plant Spirit Magic and Healing
Friend In Need - Wizard Zittle, 1830s
Grass Root Words - poetry

*